Supporting Beginning
English Teachers

Supporting Beginning English Teachers

Research and Implications for Teacher Induction

Thomas M. McCann
Community High School, West Chicago, Illinois

Larry R. Johannessen
Northern Illinois University

Bernard P. Ricca
Dominican University

National Council of Teachers of English
1111 W. Kenyon Road, Urbana, Illinois 61801-1096

Staff Editor: Bonny Graham
Interior Design: Jenny Jensen Greenleaf
Cover Design: Pat Mayer

NCTE Stock Number: 02697

Library of Congress Cataloging-in-Publication Data

McCann, Thomas M.
    Supporting beginning English teachers : research and implications for teacher induction / Thomas M. McCann, Larry R. Johannessen, Bernard P. Ricca.
        p. cm.
    Includes bibliographical references and index.
    ISBN 0-8141-0269-7 (pbk.)
    1. English teachers—United States—Attitudes. 2. English teachers—Employment—United States. 3. English philology—Vocational guidance. 4. Educational surveys—United States. I. Johannessen, Larry R. II. Ricca, Bernard. III. Title.
    PE68.U5M37 2005
    428'.0071—dc22
                                                            2005004738

*To all teachers, who have endured challenges to
make their contributions to the profession, and
who inspire us every day.*

CONTENTS

FOREWORD ix
Jeffrey D. Wilhelm

PREFACE xiii

ACKNOWLEDGMENTS xvii

1 The Problem of Attrition 1
2 Research Methods 8
3 Common Concerns 16
4 Follow-up 34
5 Survey Results 44
6 The Common Life of the First-Year Teacher 55
7 The Benefits of Experience 86
8 The Struggle for Experience 98
9 Steps toward Helping Beginning Teachers 118
10 Guiding New Teachers to Help Themselves 136
11 Summary of Recommendations 158
12 Directions for Future Research 163

APPENDIXES 167

BIBLIOGRAPHY 199

INDEX 207

AUTHORS 213

FOREWORD

JEFFREY D. WILHELM
Boise State University

A few days ago I was kayaking the South Branch of the Payette River in Central Idaho. I was scouting the last set of rapids called Slalom, which includes several technical turns and some tremendous waves. It was a long boiling broth of frothy whitewater, and it was hard to see a safe way down.

As I planned my "lines" through the rapids, another kayaker appeared on the horizon line of the river. "Oh good," I thought to myself, "I'll watch what lines this water dog uses."

The boater took the first drop river right, as I had also planned to do, ferried across some heavy current to avoid a hole, and then headed from river left back to river right. As he made his next turn, he was swept sideways into a huge diagonal wave.

"Uh oh," I thought. "He's toast."

At that moment, he rolled aggressively into the wave and dug his paddle straight into it. Amazingly, he came right through the wave and righted himself before the next wave in the drop. I'd never seen or heard of this move before, but it worked like a charm.

A few moments later I was headed down the drop myself. I got turned in the same trough before the same diagonal wave. I rolled into the wave and dug my paddle into it. Wow! I was ready to be rolled, rocked, and riveted, but I came right through the wave! The move had worked for me too.

Now, you might say that I was an autodidact, that I was able to teach myself how to become a more expert kayaker. I would say, "Not so." The previous kayaker had been my mentor, modeling what I needed to do so I could follow along and be apprenticed into a higher level of expertise. If he had not come downriver before my own descent, I would not have known what to do and would have certainly spent some time upside down in the raging whitewater.

George Hillocks, doctoral advisor, mentor, and powerful influence on Tom McCann and Larry Johannessen, myself, and countless other English teachers and educators, has famously proclaimed that "everything that is learned, must be taught" (Hillocks, 1995). Tharp and Gallimore (1988), in their famous study *Rousing Minds to Life*, likewise maintained that teachers, like students, need continual assistance over time to be able to improve and grow in their craft.

Luckily we have Tom McCann, Larry Johannessen, and Barney Ricca to help us with the greatest and most neglected educational challenge of our time: preparing preservice teachers for what must be one of the most exciting, complex, and rigorous professions there is, and *transitioning them* into the profession so that they avoid being overwhelmed, as so many new teachers are, and in such a way that they can be successful and grow into continually developing expertise.

Lee Shulman (1987), in his research on teacher expertise, argues that teaching successfully is much more demanding than is typically realized. He identifies seven facets of teacher knowledge that are necessary to effective teaching. Knowledge of content is only one of these facets. Others include knowledge of students, of human development, of curriculum, and of learning contexts, general pedagogical knowledge (processes and management and organizational techniques that transcend particular subject matter), and "pedagogical content knowledge," in other words, understanding *how* to assist learners to deeply understand and make use of particular disciplinary-specific knowledge structures, content, and procedures for operating on and using this content. Pam Grossman (1990) has shown that teachers who do not possess and use these kinds of knowledge are unsuccessful and often leave the profession. Teaching is indeed complex. And Larry, Tom, and Barney understand teaching in all its complexity and—more important—how to help teachers deal with this complexity.

Entering into the teaching profession is a bit like approaching heavy-duty Class IV and V rapids after a long river float. It's not that the float, like university courses and student teaching, was without challenges. You could practice many of the techniques needed later on down the river, hone your skills, and build your confidence in an environment of relative safety. But when the big drops and rapids approach, a whole new level of demands is placed on your strategic repertoire—and a completely new set of consequences.

Tom McCann, Larry Johannessen, and Barney Ricca remind me of seasoned river guides. They know the river of teaching and all its vagaries, pitfalls, holes, and descents. They know the moves and the strokes to expertly navigate teaching's many challenges. They know how to "play safety" and to complete midriver rescues when things go astray, as they sometimes do in this most human of all professions.

Tom, Larry, and Barney know that teaching requires profound competence, a reflective turn of mind, and systems of support. They understand the rich repertoires of strategies that expert teachers must develop in many different areas: relating to students and parents; navigating school cultures; understanding adolescent development; and knowing how to teach reading, writing, speaking, listening, multimedia design, and much more. They know that teaching is hard and that risk taking and failure are part of being a successful teacher. Even a good river runner swims sometimes. Even the best baseball team can only hope to win two of three. If they do, they go to the World Series and perhaps win the biggest prize of all. But good athletes, like good teachers, learn from their prior experience to develop an ever-wider repertoire of strategies and supports to be used in the future.

Tom, Larry, and Barney not only understand the complexity of teaching well in an individual classroom, but they also understand teaching well in a wider cultural context. They understand how to factor in demands like those placed on us by the pressures of standardized testing, mandated curricula, behavioral issues, and the like.

I've long admired Tom and Larry's work. I've seen both work with students: they are humane and relational, and think as deeply as anyone I know about what it takes to be a successful teacher. They push their students hard in the kindest possible ways; they push themselves even harder.

You can always be sure that their work as researchers and writers will be careful, cogent, insightful, and very, very fine. I use several of their previous texts in my work with both inservice and preservice teachers. I'm grateful to both for their passion, for their hard thinking, for their innovative practices—all grounded in the reality of teaching and the authority of their own experiences. For this text, Barney Ricca has joined the effort to expand our knowledge about the realities of teaching and to invite us to think about our responsibilities to encourage and sustain those who are new to the profession.

If I were headed down the river of teaching for the first time, I would want these three as my trip captains. I would want them to be showing me my lines and moves. I'd want them playing safety. I've used McCann and Johannessen this way for many years now as I've helped preservice teachers. This wonderful book will give these three teacher-authors a wider audience for whom they can perform these same pedagogical services. I recommend all of their work to you, but particularly this volume, with the highest possible regard. When you take a learning journey with these thinkers, you can be sure that you will learn more than you imagined and that you will have lots of hard and significant fun in the process. I can't think of a higher recommendation than that. Read this book. It will enrich your understanding of teaching and how to assist yourself and others to wield more pedagogical power.

Works Cited

Grossman, P. L. (1990). *The making of a teacher: Teacher knowledge and teacher education.* New York: Teachers College Press.

Hillocks, G., Jr. (1995). *Teaching writing as reflective practice.* New York: Teachers College Press.

Shulman, L. S. (1987). Knowledge and teaching: Foundations of the new reform. *Harvard Educational Review, 57*(1), 1–22.

Tharp, R. G., and Gallimore, R. (1988). *Rousing minds to life: Teaching, learning, and schooling in social context.* Cambridge: Cambridge University Press.

PREFACE

Beginning teachers are exposed to many challenges and difficulties; as a result, nearly half will leave teaching within their first five years in the profession. Previous research has identified a number of critical challenges facing new teachers. Our book reports on a study that extends the earlier research about the concerns of beginning teachers in general and also examines specifically the concerns of beginning high school English teachers. Although the book reviews the common concerns among beginning English teachers and the underlying factors that make these concerns distressful, we also describe the new teachers' means for coping with difficulties, their journey toward competence and confidence, and the measures that universities, schools, and the new teachers themselves can take to increase the likelihood that promising new teachers will remain in the profession.

One noteworthy study of teacher retention (Boe, Bobbitt, Cook, Whitener, and Weber, 1996) looks at the characteristics of teachers and their teaching assignment to offer predictors of teacher retention. The authors note that the teachers most likely to remain on the job from one year to the next fit this profile: age thirty-nine to fifty-five; married, with dependent children above age five; placed in a full-time assignment for which he or she is highly qualified; and receives a competitive salary. The problem is that few schools can remain within the constraints of these criteria in hiring new teachers. In fact, school districts facing financial challenges would look for candidates who distinctly contrast with this profile. And what schools today are not facing financial difficulties? Schools, then, are left to hire new teachers who are by definition at high risk of leaving the profession before attaining tenure.

No Dream Denied, a report of the National Commission on Teaching and America's Future (2003), concludes, "It is as if we were pouring teachers into a bucket with a fist-sized hole in the bottom" (p. 21). The startling image captures the state of attrition that outpaces the rate of preparing new teachers and sending them into classrooms. The monumental challenge facing teacher preparation programs and schools is to overcome the factors that cause attrition and find strategic new ways to reduce frustrations and elevate the rewards, the mission, and the obligations of teaching.

Organization

This book has three major parts: (1) We begin with a report of the major concerns of beginning high school English teachers from city and suburban schools. The report is based on sets of interviews with novice teachers and follow-up interviews with some of the same teachers after a year or two of experience. (2) Next we explore the differences between new teachers and experienced teachers. Through the use of survey data, interviews with experienced teachers, contrasting responses to problem teaching scenarios, and an analysis of three case studies of beginning teachers, we illustrate the underlying difficulties that new teachers face in trying to fashion a teacher persona. This section of the book includes a description of a common pattern of experience for the first-year high school English teacher. (3) The third and most expansive part of the book reviews several means that research findings suggest as useful for supporting new teachers in their induction to the profession. This section reviews steps that teacher preparation programs at colleges and universities can take to equip the newly minted teacher to have a successful experience in the classroom. We recommend actions that schools can take to support the retention of beginning teachers during their formative years of service, and we propose the steps that universities and schools can take in tandem to help the new teachers survive and thrive. In addition, we offer suggestions for the actions that new teachers can take to help themselves.

The beginning teachers we interviewed reported their greatest concerns about teaching and described their strategies for contending with difficult situations in school. While the teachers report a variety of personal concerns, we do detect some general trends in underlying factors causing the new teachers' frustrations. The interviews reveal patterns of speech for those who are likely to stay in teaching and for those who are likely to leave teaching. The patterns that we note and the specific advice from the new teachers suggest ways that schools can help to retain early career teachers.

The study reveals that while new teachers can identify veteran teachers whom they see as models, the beginners find it difficult to be like the teachers they admire. It is clear that the development into becoming a confident and highly competent teacher is a slow process that involves shaping a public self. Through the use of case studies of three first-year teachers and through the contrast between new teachers' and experienced teachers' responses to a set of problem-based teaching situations, we explore some differences between new and experienced teachers, and we report some of the difficulties that new teachers have in becoming more like the teachers they recognize as skilled and admirable.

The testimonies of beginning teachers illustrate the troubles these teachers face as they begin their careers. We use the identification of concerns as a guide for probing the underlying factors in the teachers' frustrations and as a framework for suggesting the means that schools, universities, and new teachers themselves can take to support the growth and retention of emerging educators.

Uses of This Book

Several groups should have an interest in this book, and each group will probably gravitate to a different aspect of the study. University instructors and supervisors will want to be aware of the issues that concern new teachers in order to direct their preparation and supervision toward equipping novices to contend with predictable difficulties. School leaders, especially those with responsibility for the supervision and mentoring of new teachers, will want to be aware of the concerns of beginning teachers, their coping strategies, the signs of someone's imminent exit from teaching, and the steps that school personnel can take to influence teachers to stay and grow. We anticipate that aspects of this study will help teacher educators to project what is likely in store for prospective teachers as they begin teaching. Later chapters of the book can help university instructors and school supervisors to prepare newcomers to the profession to take the steps they need to help themselves grow and thrive in their new careers as English teachers.

In short, we expect that teacher trainers, mentors, and supervisors will all find something of value in this book. Ideally, all of the groups will become familiar with the research about the concerns of beginning teachers so that training, mentoring, and supervision draw from a research base rather than from experience and intuition alone.

The research reveals the complexity of possible solutions to teacher retention. The mission of supporting new teachers is not the sole charge of any individual institution, but is instead a community effort that involves partnerships between teacher education programs, cooperating schools, and the schools that employ new teachers.

We expect also that this report might be of some use to educators who pursue their own research about the induction and retention of new teachers. We hope that the current work raises some new questions and suggests some methodologies that prove useful in learning more about the pressures that drive newcomers away from teaching and about the factors that can encourage retention.

ACKNOWLEDGMENTS

Over three years we conducted the several phases of research that we report in this book. Like most research, this work could not have been done without the support and participation of numerous contributors. First of all, although we will not name our subjects or identify their institutions, we offer deep gratitude to the many teachers, new and experienced, who sacrificed time from busy schedules to allow us to interview them. In some instances, the teachers opened their classrooms to allow us to observe them at their craft. We also thank the supervisors and administrators in the schools that allowed us to interview staff and observe in the classrooms. To the many preservice and experienced teachers who completed a fairly lengthy survey, we also express our gratitude. We are indebted to the generous contributions of time and reflection from the many teachers we met; we can reward them only with the promise that the current research might benefit future teachers as they enter and develop in the classroom. In addition to the subjects whose testimonies and other responses are represented in the book, we need to thank other teachers whom we interviewed but whose testimonies are not included in the report.

Several colleagues assisted in the collection of data and in the preparation for analysis. We would especially like to thank Linda Brandt, Nicole Haley, Beth Hunter, Cheri Petty, Monica Piszczek, and Manda Scruggs; Manda Scruggs deserves special mention for her insightful and useful comments regarding first- and second-year teachers. Stephanie Townsend was especially helpful in providing guidance and support for the statistical analyses. We appreciate also the clerical support that Tammy Henry has provided. Christopher Lapeyre and Michele Lapeyre were instrumental in piloting the survey instrument and guiding us in its refinement.

At several stages in the process of interpreting the data and pondering their implications, we were assisted by our insightful colleagues Kathleen Benton, Susan Callahan, Alan C. Jones, and Elizabeth Kahn. Other colleagues made our way easier through their advice and through their logistical support, including Judith Barford, Dianne Chambers, Fred Hamel, Jeffrey Kargol, Dwayne Kovack, and Salina Shrofel.

In a broader sense, we have relied on the support of colleagues who have dedicated themselves to the training of English teachers. We would especially like to thank Dianne Chambers and Paula Ressler. We acknowledge also the assistance of dedicated teachers Greg Leitner and Andrew Boque, who have worked to make the induction into teaching a rewarding challenge for newcomers. We need to thank also William Stone and the Illinois Association of Teacher Educators for their support through a research grant, and the Illinois Association for Supervision and Curriculum Development for their support through the Winn Research Award.

We have made it a habit of relying on the advice and careful reading of Joseph M. Flanagan, George Hillocks Jr., Elizabeth Kahn, Pamela G. McCann, Judy Minor, Peter Smagorinsky, Michael W. Smith, and Jeff Wilhelm. They have offered valuable suggestions throughout the research process. We have relied on them to read chapters and to offer commentary. Their generous efforts have guided us in making the written report more organized and readable.

Throughout a three-year process of visiting schools and interviewing subjects, we have enjoyed the patient support of the leadership at our institutions. We would especially like to thank LeRoy Rieck, John Highland, Gail Arnoff, and Kim Chambers for seeing the value in this work and giving us the support and encouragement to complete it.

We would like to thank NCTE Senior Editor Zarina Hock. First, we are indebted to Dr. Hock for her unwavering support from initial conception of the project to its final product. We have also gained much from her editorial efforts throughout a long process.

We are indebted to the NCTE editorial staff, and to Bonny Graham in particular, for her careful and insightful reading of the manuscript and for her masterful work in shaping our rough efforts into a much more coherent text.

CHAPTER ONE

The Problem of Attrition

In a sense, we began this study by writing a book (Johannessen & McCann, 2002). For years we have been principally responsible for the preparation, inservice training, and supervision of high school English teachers. Guided by our concern that beginning teachers often enter the profession without a realistic sense of the challenges that are likely to confront them, we began work on a casebook that would prompt discussions and lead teachers to develop the strategic and critical thinking skills that could help them to avoid or endure difficulties inherent in teaching. After more than twenty-five years of teaching, we believed that we had a clear idea of the kind of challenges that would seriously frustrate new teachers. Although we thought we knew about the chief concerns of beginning teachers, we decided we had better ask. Former Speaker of the U.S. House of Representatives, Thomas "Tip" O'Neill, recalled that his long-time neighbor expected him to ask her for her vote, even though he thought he could take her vote for granted. She counseled O'Neill, "let me tell you something: people like to be asked" (O'Neill, 1987, p. 26). Before we proceeded with the casebook, we recognized that it would be not only polite but also prudent to ask beginning teachers about their concerns and about their strategies for remaining committed to teaching.

We began by interviewing the student teachers and other beginning teachers to whom we had immediate access. A somewhat casual process of conversation led to a more deliberate program of investigation. Our initial interviews highlighted two clear generalizations: (1) beginning teachers often have a difficult time; and (2) beginning teachers need help in coping with the difficulties they encounter during their induction into teaching. We could hear the distress in the responses of the beginning teachers, and we could recall seeing other teachers' expressions of frustration during their initial years of teaching. The responses reminded us of Whyte's (1948) sociological study about what makes waitresses cry. He reports that waitresses, caught in the middle between the demands of the customers and the expectations of managers and kitchen staff, often feel unremitting stress. Using different methodology, and with a different purpose in mind, we sought to learn what gives beginning teachers the greatest concern, and we hoped to prompt purposeful discussion about ways to ease the pain of the induction process.

As we planned to interview other beginning teachers and to survey both beginning and experienced teachers, we kept in mind two broad research questions:

1. What are the significant frustrations that could influence beginning teachers to leave the profession?

2. What supports, resources, and preparations influence beginning teachers to remain in the profession?

In the current climate of teacher shortages and rapid teacher turnover, it is critical for schools and teacher preparation programs to be able to answer these questions and to prepare to act on the directions the answers suggest.

The Impact of Teacher Shortages

Various sources point to trends in school enrollment data and project a continuing teacher shortage (Darling-Hammond, 1997, 2000; Henke, et al., 1997; Texas State Board of Education, 1998). Hussar (1999b) projects that between 1998–99 and 2008–09, public schools will need to hire 2.4 million new teachers (p. 9). Furthermore, under one scenario that recognizes increasing enrollment and efforts at class size reduction, the projected need would grow to 2.7 million.

The data suggest that a main contributor to future teacher shortages will be a change in demographics: many teachers will retire in the next ten years (Hussar, 1999a; Gerald & Hussar, 1998). A smaller pool of qualified new teachers is prepared to replace the retirees. Henke and colleagues (1997) report that only about half of those teachers who train to teach actually apply for teaching jobs. Darling-Hammond (1997) reports that little has changed since 1991, when approximately 25 percent of all secondary teachers did not have the appropriate subject area training to teach in the field to which they were assigned. And while many teachers are leaving the profession, high school enrollments continue to grow (Educational Resources Information Center, 1998).

Ingersoll (2002) and Ingersoll and Smith (2003) report that more people than ever are in colleges and universities preparing to become teachers. According to their analyses, the problem of teacher shortages is not so much a problem of retirements outpacing the preparation of new teachers as it is a problem of new teachers leaving the profession in such numbers and so rapidly that the newcomers do not stay around long enough to fill the vacancies for the long haul. A report of the National Commission on Teaching & America's Future (2003) concludes, "It is as if we were pouring teachers into a bucket with a fist-sized hole in the bottom" (p. 8). Merrow (1999) observes, "The teaching pool keeps losing water because no one is paying attention to the leak. That is, we're misdiagnosing the problem as 'recruitment' when it's really retention" (p. 64). The popular leaking resources metaphor reveals the frustrating difficulty of retaining the critically valuable new teachers who have spent much time to prepare for teaching and who offer much promise for the future of schools.

Teacher shortages are exacerbated when new teachers leave the profession after just a few years. According to Perez, Swain, and Hartsough (1997), 30 percent of beginning teachers leave the profession within their first two years of teaching. Darling-Hammond (2000) notes that the rate of attrition among teachers in their first two years of teaching is at least double the average for teachers overall. Attrition appears to hit hardest those teachers at the beginning of their careers. Hussar (1999b) notes: "Newly minted teachers and returning teachers have lower continuation rates than those of the same age who had been teaching the previous year. If the proportion of new teachers in the teaching force grows over time, it would tend to push continuation rates downward" (p. 6). Hussar's (1999a, 1999b) analysis suggests that when attrition rates grow, shortages will increase.

Causes of Teacher Attrition

Several studies report the many reasons for teachers leaving the profession. Hussar's (1999b) analysis suggests that within the next ten years teachers will be retiring from public schools in great numbers. In 1999 "there were more public school teachers age 46 than any other age" (p. 5). He also reports that most teachers retire before they turn sixty: "53 percent of those in their fifties retired; and over 90 percent of teachers 60 years and over retired" (p. 6). Hussar (1999a) anticipates that between 1998–99 and 2008–09, between 745,000 and 765,000 teachers will retire.

Ingersoll (2001, 2002) and Ingersoll and Smith (2003) note that factors other than retirement account for much of the turnover among teachers. Teachers leaving the profession cite job dissatisfaction and other job opportunities as key factors that influenced the change. The departing teachers cite as the primary sources of their job dissatisfaction "student discipline problems; lack of support from the school administration; poor student motivation; and lack of teacher influence over schoolwide and classroom decision making" (Ingersoll & Smith, 2003, p. 32). Whitener and colleagues (1997) also found that student discipline problems, poor student motivation to learn, and inadequate support from administration were the most often cited reasons for teachers' dissatisfaction.

Teacher attrition is a serious problem. Schools endure a fiscal cost when they lose a teacher. According to a study conducted by the Texas Teacher Certification Board, when a teacher leaves a district during the "induction years" of teaching, it costs the taxpayers about $50,000 (Texas State Board of Education, 1998). The board measured the costs by considering the investment in preparation, recruitment and hiring, and professional development and supervisory support.

The rapid turnover of teachers affects learning. Even the most well-prepared and uncommonly gifted and mature beginning teacher is still a novice at the profession. One can imagine parents' concern if their children were to encounter a "newly minted" teacher in one subject area every year for four years of high school.

A rapid teacher turnover erodes public confidence in schools. Both schools and learners experience a lack of continuity.

Some causes of the early departure of teachers from the profession are beyond the control or influence of teacher preparation programs or of the schools. According to Wayne (2000), 44 percent of beginning teachers who leave teaching cite personal and family reasons as the key factors. If teachers leave because of changes in family obligations, a spouse's job transfer, or the winning of the lottery, there is nothing a teacher preparation program or a school can do to influence retention. But if teacher training programs and schools can recognize the sources of serious concerns and frustrations among beginning teachers, perhaps they can develop some interventions that will influence a greater percentage of new teachers to remain long enough to become veteran teachers and in the process become highly skilled and confident teachers.

A change in the policies of school districts and individual schools might offer some promise for keeping beginning teachers in the profession beyond their period of induction. Attractive salaries and fringe benefits and pleasant working conditions might influence teachers to endure the challenges that frustrate them (Whitener, et al., 1997). It is a cruel reality that beginning teachers often receive the most difficult teaching assignments, with multiple preparations, the sharing of classrooms, and classes with the most difficult students. Changes in these common practices might improve job satisfaction among beginning teachers.

Grossman, Thompson, and Valencia (2001) observe that district policy has an impact on the satisfaction and encouragement of beginning teachers. They conclude that the policies school districts follow will greatly influence the new teacher's experience: "The tasks they assign new teachers, the resources they provide, the learning environments they create, the assessments they design, and the conversations they provoke have consequences for what these first year teachers come to learn about teaching the language arts, and about teaching more generally" (p. 19). The study emphasizes that the particular setting for teaching will contribute to defining the new teacher's experience and will support or frustrate the new teacher, who will inevitably contend with challenges.

Concerns of Beginning Teachers

The influential work of Fuller (1969) and later work by Rutherford and Hall (1990) reveal that beginning teachers have serious concerns about managing classrooms, about being viewed as credible professionals by their colleagues and by parents, about being liked and accepted by students, and about being evaluated by supervisors. Borko and Putnam (1996) and Veenman (1984) also report that beginning teachers struggle with identifying effective approaches to classroom management, defining themselves as teachers, and finding meaningful ways to teach their subject. Preservice and beginning teachers also worry about how they will grade students, how they will respond to challenges about grades, and how they will handle a monumental workload. Preservice teachers also commonly express concerns about having the freedom to put into practice the concepts and beliefs about teaching they have embraced during their college or university training.

The previous research about teachers' concerns points to a number of problem areas. New data, in the form of interview and survey responses, reveal some patterns that underlie all the concerns that might, at first glance, seem rather disparate.

Research Questions

The current study focuses on the kinds of concerns with which teacher training and professional development programs can assist teachers in coping. Rather than preparing a laundry list of teacher concerns, we seek to identify common causes for the variety of frustrations that new teachers experience. We focus on the sources of frustration that might influence a teacher to leave the profession before attaining tenure. In the study, we seek to answer these questions:

1. What are the significant frustrations that could influence beginning teachers to leave the profession?

2. What are the factors that underlie the frustrations?

3. What supports, resources, and preparation influence beginning teachers to remain in the profession at least until they attain tenure?

We address the first two questions through several research methods, which we describe in the following chapter. In later chapters, we trace a general pattern of development for teachers' first year and after several years of teaching. We also explore the steps toward supporting the growth of beginning teachers that the research findings suggest need to be taken.

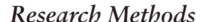

Research Methods

Research Procedures

To investigate our questions about teachers' concerns and their means for coping, we collected data in six stages: (1) we interviewed a series of beginning teachers and produced the transcripts from the interviews; (2) we surveyed preservice and practicing teachers about their anticipated and actual experience in teaching; (3) we conducted follow-up interviews with six of the original eleven teachers we had interviewed; (4) we tracked the progress of three first-year teachers over the course of one school year; (5) we conducted interviews with six experienced teachers; and (6) from six beginning teachers and their mentors, we solicited responses to a set of seven problem-based scenarios. Descriptions of each stage of data collection follow.

Initial Interviews

Over a two-year period, we interviewed three student teachers and eight other novice teachers. All the teachers taught English in a high school. Those we label *novice* teachers each had less than five years of teaching experience. The first five years of teaching appear to be a vulnerable time. In some states, teachers do not earn tenure until they have completed four years of continuous service, making the first four years of teaching probationary. We use the term *novice* here to designate nontenured teachers, and we use the term interchangeably with other terms and phrases such as *beginners, newcomers, newly minted, early career*. We do not mean to indicate that "novice" designates a specific developmental stage.

In all, we initially interviewed eleven teachers. The first six interviewees were working at a large, diverse suburban high school: two student teachers, one first-year teacher, one second-year teacher, one person in his third year of teaching, and one person in her fourth year of teaching. We also interviewed five more teachers from two other schools, to represent the experiences of high school English teachers in a variety of settings. Three of these interviewees were from an inner-core city high school in a large public school system. One of the three teachers was a student teacher at the time of the first interview. Two interviewees were from a suburban high school with a substantial minority population.

Seven of the subjects for the initial phase of the research were female and four were male. Ten of the subjects were white, and one was African American. The proportion of female to male and white to minority reflects the prevailing ratio in the teaching profession as a whole (Snyder & Hoffman, 2003; Henke, Chen, & Geis, 2000).

The student population at the one urban school had the following ethnic composition: 50 percent African American, 40 percent Latino and Asian, and 10 percent white. Each of the two suburban schools had a significant minority population. The minority population, mostly Latino, at one of the suburban high schools constituted 40 percent of the enrollment. At the other high school, the minority population, mostly Latino and Asian, constituted approximately 35 percent of the enrollment.

The questions that were the basis for the interviews appear as Appendix A. In each case, we asked the interviewee to focus on his or her experiences from the first year of teaching. For the student teachers, the focus was on their student teaching experience. All the interviews were collected on audiotape and transcribed. The transcribed interviews were returned to interviewees so that they could check for any inaccuracies, and we subsequently edited and corrected the transcripts before doing any analysis.

Following the methodology suggested by Erickson (1986), we read the transcripts of all the interviews several times and independently wrote a summary of the trends across the set of eleven interviews. Three other readers studied the same set of transcripts and produced summaries, or "conceptual memos."

Each of these readers had a doctorate in education: two with an emphasis in curriculum and instruction, one with an emphasis in educational administration. The following questions guided the readers in producing the memos: (1) Among the set of interviews, what do the teachers' concerns have in common? Although all the stressful situations will be different, what *common underlying factors* cause the stress? (2) Can you identify a *pattern of ways* that the teachers have *managed to cope* with the stressful situations? (3) In general, how have the novice teachers *sought and used help* that might be available in the school? Did they believe that help was available? (4) In general, what observations do the teachers offer about ways in which teacher education programs can *better prepare* beginning teachers to anticipate and manage the stresses and frustrations of the job? (5) Note also any *other insights* that you can provide.

We reviewed the set of summaries to find common observations about the trends in interviewees' comments about factors that caused stress, the methods for coping with stressful situations, and the preparation and support for teaching. The initial analysis of the interviews suggested that much of the frustration beginning teachers feel derives from experiences that are drastically different from the ways they had anticipated teaching would be. To examine if this contrast between the anticipation and the actual experience was the source of the frustration, we surveyed preservice and practicing teachers, using survey statements that varied only in their verb tense, from future (anticipated) to present (actual).

Surveys of Preservice and Practicing Teachers

We constructed two surveys that differ only in the shift in verb tense from present to future. Each survey offers a series of statements, and prompts the respondents to indicate the extent to which each statement accurately expresses the subject's experience as a teacher or the anticipated experience. We labeled the survey for the preservice teachers the "Teacher Expectation Survey" and the survey for the practicing teachers the "Teacher Experience Survey." The surveys appear as Appendixes B and C, respectively. The preservice teachers responded to statements that predicted what their experience as teachers *will be* in the future. One statement, for example, notes, "The parents of my students will appreciate the efforts I am making to serve and support their children." The practicing teacher's form for the same survey reads: "The parents of my students appreciate the efforts I am making to serve and support their children."

In a pilot phase, we administered the surveys to five preservice teachers and five practicing teachers. After the subjects responded to the surveys, we interviewed the subjects to discover any problems they experienced with the instruments. The subjects commented on the clarity of the instructions, the focus of each item, and the distinctiveness of each response choice. The respondents' comments guided us in adjusting the surveys.

We then administered the Teacher Expectation Survey to twenty-five preservice (undergraduate and graduate) teachers and the Teacher Experience Survey to twenty practicing teachers. A split-halves test of reliability indicated that the scales are reliable.

After we confirmed that the survey instruments satisfied tests of validity and reliability, the surveys were administered to two groups of subjects. The Teacher Expectation Survey was sent to preservice English teachers at six universities. Five of the universities were large state schools with many students enrolled in English methods classes. Two of these universities were located in large metropolitan areas. Two of the universities were located in the South, one in the Northeast, and two in the Midwest. A total of 218 preservice teachers responded to the surveys.

The Teacher Experience Survey was administered to English department faculty members at six high schools in the Midwest. All of the schools were public high schools. One was a small school in a rural area, and five were large high schools in suburban communities. A total of 141 teachers responded.

Follow-up Interviews

In all, we conducted six follow-up interviews with teachers who contributed to the initial set of eleven interviews. One subject was interviewed during her student teaching experience and then interviewed a second time at the end of her first year of teaching. Two subjects were interviewed at the end of their second year of teaching and interviewed again after their third year. Another subject was interviewed after her second year of teaching at one school, and then again two years later, in her second year at another school. One subject was interviewed after his first year of teaching and interviewed again at the end of his third year, after he had resigned from his teaching position. One subject was interviewed after his second year of teaching, and then a second time after he had been away from teaching for a year. The summary in Table 2.1 outlines the breakdown of the subjects for the follow-up interviews.

The follow-up interviews were less elaborate than the first occasions, focusing on four general areas. The questions used in the follow-up interviews appear as Appendix D. Four of the interviews were conducted in person, with the interviewer recording and transcribing the observations. In each case, the interviewer read the transcript aloud to the interviewee to allow for corrections and clarification. Two of the interviews were conducted via e-mail, so the interviewee typed and transmitted the responses.

The follow-up interviews tracked changes in the experiences of the novice teachers over a year or two. The questions asked the teachers to explain what kept them in teaching so far and what would help to keep them in teaching in the future. We also asked two of the subjects why they left teaching and what would bring them back to teaching in the future.

TABLE 2.1. Summary of Follow-up Interviews

Subject	First Interview	Second Interview	Still Teaching?
1	Student Teaching	First Year	Yes
2	Second Year	Third Year	Yes
3	Second Year	Third Year	Yes
4	Second Year	Fourth Year	Yes
5	First Year	Third Year	No
6	Second Year	Year after Resignation	No

Each of us read the transcripts of the follow-up interviews independently and then wrote our observations about the patterns of speech that seem to distinguish the teachers who stay from the teachers who leave the profession. We then discussed our separate findings together to narrow our observations to a set of common statements. We report the general trends and the underlying factors for many concerns in the following chapter.

Other Methods

The initial phases of the study prompted additional research questions, requiring additional means for the collection and analysis of data. We describe here three sets of procedures we used for gaining insight into the experience of beginning high school English teachers.

Our initial interviews and the follow-up interviews revealed beginning teachers' greatest concerns and their means for enduring the difficulties they faced. We wondered if the critical periods in a first-year teacher's experience occurred at particular times during the school year. Having a sense of the pattern of experience of the typical first-year high school English teacher would inform teacher preparation, equip the new teacher with knowledge about what to expect, and allow mentors and supervisors to anticipate critical times. We tracked the progress of three first-year high school English teachers during the course of one complete school year. The teachers worked in three different schools, all fairly large suburban high schools. We conducted a series of interviews and classroom observations with the new teachers. We visited and observed the teacher's class twice during the year. Table 2.2 provides a schedule of these visits. After the interviews and observations were completed, we each produced a case study of the subject. The three of us read all the case studies and identified common trends. We then discussed our observations to generalize about a pattern of experience over the course of a school year.

The survey data from preservice and experienced teachers revealed distinct differences between the two groups. We questioned what happened to experienced teachers over time that

TABLE 2.2. Schedule of Visits for First-Year Teachers

September:	Initial interview: What classes are you teaching? What are your impressions of the school and the students? What has been the high point of your experience so far? What challenges do you face and what concerns do you have at this point? What support do you have in the school to help you face challenges? To what extent do you rely on help from outside the school? How well has your college or university program prepared you for your current teaching experience?
Late October:	Interview and classroom observation: How have you been able to contend with the curriculum you have been assigned to teach? How much time do you typically spend each day, and on weekends, to prepare for lessons and to grade papers? How has the workload affected you? General impressions from the lesson observed: classroom management/rapport, knowledge, pedagogy.
December:	Third interview: Are there changes from the original responses? What has been the high point of your experience so far? What challenges do you face and what concerns do you have at this point? What support do you have in the school to help you face challenges? To what extent do you rely on help from outside the school? How well has your college or university program prepared you for your current teaching experience?
Early March:	Fourth interview: Focus on supervision/teacher evaluation. Describe your rapport with your supervisor(s). Describe the teacher evaluation process. To what extent does the teacher evaluation program support your professional development? To what extent have your colleagues been helpful in supporting your development as a teacher? To what extent has your teaching experience changed during the course of the school year: relationship with students, colleagues, supervisors, parents; handling workload; command of subject/curriculum, grading/assessment, autonomy? Second observation: what changes do you perceive from the first to the second observation?
Late May:	Fifth interview: As you reflect on your first year of teaching, what were the most memorable experiences? What were the greatest challenges? What advice would you offer to someone who was beginning his or her first year of teaching? What advice would you offer school administrators to guide their efforts toward supporting new teachers and encouraging retention? What advice would you offer the directors of teacher training programs to prepare new teachers to enter and remain in the profession?

would account for the distinctions. We interviewed six experienced teachers about the areas that the survey data revealed as showing significant differences. The interview questions asked the experienced teachers to explain how they had changed over time and to describe the factors that influenced the change. We produced transcripts of the six interviews. Again, three outside readers studied the transcripts and wrote conceptual memos to note common trends among the experienced teachers.

We sought also to discover how beginning teachers are distinct from experienced teachers, especially in shaping who they are as teachers. To explore this topic, we produced seven scenarios that embedded major concerns of beginning teachers. The scenarios appear in Appendixes E and F. The protocol for this stage of the research included these steps: (1) Each of us individually provided six first-year teachers with the scenarios and asked each teacher to write an explanation of how he or she would respond if faced with the same difficulty. (2) We asked each first-year teacher to identify someone in his or her department that the beginning teacher recognized as a very good teacher. (3) We met with the experienced teachers that the first-year teachers identified and asked each of them to write responses to the same set of scenarios the first-year teachers had responded to. The experienced teachers wrote three responses: (a) how they would have responded to the situation during the first year of teaching; (b) how they would respond to the situation now; and (c) how they would explain any differences between the initial response and the current response. (4) We shared with each first-year teacher the experienced teacher's current response to the problem situation. In the related interview, if the first-year teacher noted any differences between the projected actions of the experienced teacher and his or her own projected actions, the first-year teacher offered an explanation of the differences.

Common Concerns

The General Trends

The quality of a new teacher's experience and the specific concerns and frustrations of each beginner will depend on a number of factors that will be unique to the specific teaching situation. A new teacher's experience will be defined in part by the beginner's preservice training, by the quality of support within a school, and by the match between the school environment and the teacher's disposition. Although each situation will be unique, it is helpful, as a beginning point, to recognize general trends. It would be useful to those training prospective teachers, to those mentoring and supervising beginning teachers, and to the new teachers themselves to be familiar with some common concerns among the beginners. For trainers, mentors, and supervisors, being able to anticipate concerns and frustrations allows them to plan supports. For beginning teachers themselves, the familiarity with common concerns allows them to gauge how usual or unusual their teaching experience is. At the same time, we recognize that the common concerns are only part of the story, because each new teacher's experience in a particular classroom and in a specific school will have its own unique character.

The interviews with eleven novice teachers support earlier research about the concerns of beginning teachers. Based on the analysis of the interview transcripts, we identify the major concerns of novice teachers under six general headings and nine categories overall. The general headings are Relationships, Workload/ Time Management, Knowledge of Subject/Curriculum, Evaluation/Grading, Autonomy/Control, and Physical/Personal Characteristics. Under the Relationships heading, we have identified four subcategories: Relationship with Students, Relationship with

Parents, Relationship with Colleagues, and Relationship with Supervisors. The list of issues and their related reflective questions appear in Table 3.1. Classroom management is also a predictable concern of beginning teachers; we see this issue as part of the larger concern about relationships with students. The discussion that follows cites interviewee testimony to illustrate some of the concerns, but we emphasize those issues that the five readers of the transcripts identified as common factors in difficulties and frustrations, and the patterns of the means that the teachers used to cope with difficult situations.

The analyses of interview transcripts suggest that a major difficulty beginning teachers face is the challenge to define for themselves their *teacher persona*. One of the readers noted that the teachers report difficulty with "constructing an authentic self . . . in an organizational structure where first-year teachers are overwhelmed by a teaching assignment that requires too many preparations, too many classes, and too many classrooms." Before entering teaching, novice teachers have assumed many roles—son/daughter, student, employee—but the role of teacher is a new one. They apparently struggle with questions such as the following: How am I *supposed to* act in this situation? How do *real teachers* do this? Am I aggressive enough in contending with management challenges? Am I overreacting? Am I insisting on unreasonable standards? Am I being too lax? These are the kinds of questions that must be answered over time and by means of comparing one's behavior against a recognizable and legitimate standard.

To illustrate the pattern of concerns and the common difficulties, we cite from the initial interviews with eleven early career teachers, including three student teachers. The three student teachers reported on their student teaching experience. The other eight subjects focused on their first year of teaching. The demographics for the group of teachers and the school populations where they worked are described in greater detail in Chapter 2.

Throughout this book, we have assigned pseudonyms to preserve the anonymity of the participants in the study. Here is the way a first-year teacher we call Jonas expresses the difficulty of determining who he is going to be as a teacher:

CHAPTER THREE

TABLE 3.1. Major Concerns of Novice Teachers

Issue	Reflective Questions
Relationships:	
Relationship with Students:	Will students like me? Will they accept that I am a bona fide teacher?
Relationship with Parents:	What will I do if a parent is upset with me? Will parents accept me as a legitimate teacher?
Relationship with Colleagues:	Will my colleagues believe that I know what I am doing? Will they respect my efforts?
Relationship with Supervisors:	Will I satisfy the expectations of an evaluator? Am I doing what "real" teachers do?
Workload/Time Management:	
Fatigue:	How can I get it all done? Do I have a life any more?
Knowledge of Subject/Curriculum:	
Focus and Framework:	In the end, what is *really* important to teach? What *principles* guide the development of the curriculum?
Evaluation/Grading:	
Value Judgments:	What am I measuring? What do I do when the numbers don't match my subjective impressions?
Autonomy/Control:	
Independence and Integrity:	Can I teach the way that I was prepared to teach, and the way that I believe is the best way to teach?
Physical/Personal Characteristics:	
Appearance and Identity:	How will my personal and physical characteristics help or inhibit me in doing my job?

I'd stay up kind of late trying to get something that I thought was really good and have sleepless nights, but in the morning I was actually . . . I'd have an almost like dry-heaving anxiety. You have to understand how strange that is for me, because normally I am a very "type B" personality: no stress whatsoever, take one thing at a time. Just having those kinds of mornings was totally strange for me. I don't think I changed eating habits or anything. I actually started out in the morning pretty well. I would wake up and have a nice breakfast. Maybe it was because . . . I was trying some new things that I didn't normally do. I kind of had to reinvent myself to do this that some of that happened, but it was just really going to school and not being 100 percent confident in what I was going to present to the students.

Jonas reports that he was a successful student throughout high school and college. His academic success promoted his confidence in his role as student. Faced with the novel situation of being the teacher, however, Jonas experienced so much doubt and conflict that he became physically ill. Part of the challenge for Jonas in reinventing himself is that he assumes he has to pretend to support a curriculum in which he is not totally invested:

It's still kind of a challenge, because I know a lot of the times that I'm not good [at] faking excitement about content that I know a lot of effective teachers do. It's just not part of my personality and I haven't developed it yet, so if I have something that I'm not totally pumped about teaching, it shows. I kind of wear my heart on my sleeve as far as that goes.

While Jonas confesses that he is not good at faking enthusiasm, he assumes other teachers are.

Although he was in his second year, a teacher we call Brendan reports on the stresses from his student teaching experience. His student teaching assignment required him to teach with a partner for four periods a day and to teach alone for one period. Like Jonas, Brendan recalls the doubts he had about fitting into his role as a teacher:

What I started to notice was, whereas the first day they [students] were sitting up straight, over the next couple of days, you could noticeably tell that they were slouching, that they were starting to slide down in their chairs a little bit, not getting eye contact. Speaking to students, learning their names, calling them by name to try to develop some kind of personal contact and [there were] a lot of shrugs, a lot of mumbling, no clear answers, never a hand up, except that one student, a lot of downcast eyes. And that really, from point one, was really tough. I felt like something was missing here.

Brendan contrasted this one frustrating class with others that he taught with a partner. In the team-teaching situation, Brendan had someone modeling teacher behavior and validating his behaviors during each class meeting. When Brendan taught alone, he contrasted the response of the one class with the responses of the other classes that he taught with a partner. He began to doubt that he was doing what accomplished teachers do.

I thought, "Boy, I don't know if I can do this, maybe I'm doing this wrong." It's the only class I had solo without a team teacher. . . . From this high coming down to this low, walking back down the hall to [the other class], which wasn't far, I just remember every once in a while thinking, "I don't know if this is going to work out. I don't know if I can do it by myself."

The difficulty in measuring up to the standard he saw in the other classes made Brendan wonder if he were cut out to be a teacher:

The ultimate doubt started to come in. . . . I started thinking, "What if I never get it? What if I just don't get it?" I think about all these thirty students. It's only one class and I think of how I have thirty years and I'll have many classes like this, and so it occupied most of my thinking.

Part of Brendan's reaction to the apparently unresponsive class was to question whether he was doing what the accomplished, experienced teachers were doing. Although he could not identify anything he was doing wrong, or anything he was doing differently from the way he operated in his other classes, he saw that the students' responses were different from one class to the next. On reflection, he judged that the only difference was the presence of an experienced teacher as a partner in the other class. Things went well when the veteran was present; lethargy appeared to set in among his students only when Brendan operated alone. He could only conclude that the fault was with him, and he had his doubts that he could grow into the model of the experienced teacher.

These excerpts from the interviews with Jonas and Brendan illustrate three recurring experiences among the novice teachers: (1) the negative episodes with one class may not represent the experience of the teacher overall; (2) the negative episodes with one class or even one student tend to taint the experience of the teacher overall; and (3) the inexperienced teacher sees the negative episodes as evidence that he or she is not doing what "bona fide" teachers do, leading to doubt about whether he or she is qualified to perform as a teacher. There appears to be a tendency among beginning teachers to fail to recognize that other teachers struggle from time to time with classroom management problems, curriculum conundrums, or other instructional challenges; and the new teachers cannot yet envision that the difficulties will diminish to an acceptable level over time.

The analyses of the interviews also reveal that frustration results in part from the significant mismatch between the teacher's *expectations* for the experience of teaching and the *realization* of the actual experience. Whether the stressful experience has to do with an unruly class, an angry parent phone call, or a supervisor's highly critical assessment of a lesson, the common element is that the experience was not what the teacher had expected. In the interviews, one student teacher, Clara, reported that her encounter with a disruptive class was a "shocker." Clara describes her frustration:

> Just an overall general sense when I went into the room every day, it was an overall sense that I am not in control of this class whatsoever, none. Feeling like that can be particularly frightening. For example, they obviously did not respect me, that's evident. They did not respect one another. They would run around, yell, scream, throw things, you name it.

The teacher describes the experience as being a "frightening" one, but her frustration resulted from the contrast between her initial belief that she knew how to manage the class and the subsequent discovery that she could not do what she thought she should. Clara characterizes the frustration in this way:

> I knew what I was supposed to be doing. I thought I knew how to do it, but their behavior was so poor. I had a real hard time dealing with it, especially that week and weeks after, because I had no experiences, no nothing. It was just like, OK, figure it out. Get some control and figure out how to do this; but it was a shocker.

Clara reports that she contended with the difficult class for weeks: "It took a long time because the things I thought would work didn't work." Clara thought about her difficult class often. In fact, when she left school and was away from the troublesome class, "I was thinking about it all the time."

Clara thought she was prepared to contend with a classroom management challenge. She had learned some strategies from education classes, and her mentor teacher could advise her; but the various strategies that she had expected would produce some results seemed to fail her. She was left with a feeling of confusion, rather than fear or anger, because she had entered an intolerable situation with the expectation that reasonable interventions would solve the problems. Clara reports that she thought she knew what to do. When the strategies that promised some success actually had little effect, she was left confused and frustrated.

Teachers can expect to encounter challenging groups of students every so often, but it would be difficult to enter the classroom every day with the belief that the students are unmanageable and that anything the teacher tries will have little effect in governing the unruly. Nadine, another of the student teachers, reports this frustrating experience: "I felt like I was pulling teeth in trying to get them to do work. I would get nervous before the class because I would always hear comments like 'This sucks' or 'Why are we doing this? I don't understand.'" Nadine did not expect that all her students would love her class and love the study of English; she had thought, however, that she could make the study of English appealing to many students. She had not anticipated a daily barrage of complaints when she was making honest efforts to provide engaging lessons.

Nadine points to another disappointment. She had referred a student to the dean when the student made what Nadine judged to be a serious physical threat toward her. The dean met with the student and then sent him to the school's learning resource center (LRC) without any corrective, intervention, or punishment, and without sending him back to the teacher's class. Nadine describes her disappointment:

> Immediately, my heart dropped because we didn't have anything going on in the LRC. He had nothing to do in there. I thought, here is something that the kid could've gotten in really serious trouble for and I felt like the repercussions should have been more stiff. I don't know if they [students] see that and think that nothing is going to happen anyway. I'm sure it's a problem at any school.

Nadine had expected support from the dean and judged that the student would likely receive an appropriate punishment. When the dean reported that he had taken an action Nadine had not expected, her "heart dropped." The perceived lack of support left her wondering how she could judge the seriousness of and appropriate response to other, similar situations. Nadine was frustrated and anxious when her expectations were not satisfied at all, and she was left to puzzle out how she should proceed in the future.

In the interviews, novice teachers report that their tasks as educators were especially fatiguing. In addition to the stress of contending with the energy and occasional resistance of adolescents during the day, the teachers spent their evenings and weekends in grading papers, responding to students' writing, completing administrative paperwork, and planning lessons. Gordon, one of the interviewees, reports that the workload was the most stressful part of the job: "I think I've had a level of stress the whole year just in terms of worrying about planning, grading, and anything like that. In order to do that, there's been a lot of twelve-, thirteen-, fourteen-hour days of work." As a first-year teacher, Gordon shared his classroom with another teacher, had several preparations, and managed a significant extracurricular activity. He reports that in his first year of teaching the job was all-consuming: "I usually work about eleven or twelve hours a day. There are other effects of that. . . .That involves giving up your whole day to that and having just moved here too and not really knowing anybody and hardly time to get out." He recognized that the current conditions in his life on a new job would dictate the investment of time:

> The people that I do know who are relatively close friends are forty-five minutes to an hour away and that is sort of a whole day trip to go there. I've taken a couple days off on weekends here and there and definitely would do that, but it's not like it's down the block where you can walk there and go shoot some pool or something. I think, "Nobody there, so I might as well grade a couple more papers."

This new teacher, who had relocated away from family and friends for the job, found himself isolated. The isolation served to define teaching as the person's sole interest and enterprise. While the teacher's isolation helped him to focus on his work, it allowed him few distractions that might have provided healthy relief from the daily routine.

The novice teachers report a variety of frustrations. The examples discussed here emphasize difficulties with managing students, planning engaging lessons, and contending with an overwhelming workload. In general, the teachers experienced frustration when they faced difficulty in defining themselves as teachers, and when their actual experience as teachers contrasted widely with what they had anticipated the job experience would be.

The Cases of Winnie and Christy

Thus far we have emphasized general trends across the experiences of all the teachers we interviewed, but we must acknowledge that the specific contexts of the teaching situations will define these experiences and cause particular persons specific kinds of difficulties. The interplay between who the individual is and where he or she teaches influences the kind of experience the novice teacher will have. Any number of factors—the age of the teacher, the physical stature and appearance of the teacher, the size and location of the school, the demographics of the student body, the administrative support for the teachers, the induction program of the school—contribute to the level and kind of stress and frustration new teachers might feel and the coping mechanisms they might invoke.

We discuss here two cases to illustrate how distinct circumstances raise special challenges. The two particular cases are noteworthy because although the experiences might seem exceptional when contrasted with those of the other nine subjects, they are likely to be the norm for many teachers in the future. The experiences of these two teachers might be characterized as the teachers' being underprepared for the school setting in which they found themselves; both teachers' physical characteristics contrasted markedly with the dominant culture of the school. As school populations across the United States become more diverse, teachers will need to understand and appreciate groups of students who, in many instances, are quite different from the teacher.

Winnie's Case

In her first year of teaching, Winnie worked in an all-male parochial high school. Winnie was petite and young, having just graduated from college. The high school had seldom employed women as teachers, making Winnie something of a rarity in the building. She reports that her youth, gender, and physical appearance and stature were all connected to the stress and discomfort she felt in her first year of teaching. First, she recalls the aggressive behavior of some students toward her:

> The older boys would whistle and catcall after me as I passed by. Some would be brazen enough to ask my age. One boy, a senior, told me he would "catch up" with me in four years. Of course, there were also the frequent stares; some would call them *leers* of nervous students. In my first few months at the school, I would have to mentally prepare and bolster myself for the long walk to my classroom.

Winnie reports that she dressed in a rather conservative fashion and had never received a similar kind of attention before. Initially, boys would leer at her in the hallways, but a few sought her attention after school in her classroom: "A group of boys even started to come to my classroom after school, and although they were only acting flirtatious in a quiet way, their presence made me feel uncomfortable and awkward." The experience occupied much of her attention and made the performance of her job difficult. She describes her emotional response in this way:

> For the first few months, I would dread cafeteria duty and the hallway walks down the hall. I would spend time thinking about the ways I could handle the situation. I felt shocked, then embarrassed, and then angry. But overall, I felt powerless. I was battling a powerful attitude of a culture with which I was unfamiliar.

The primary response was the feeling of powerlessness, which is a debilitating situation for a beginning teacher. The experience fostered a sense of hopelessness because Winnie knew she had no prospects for making the situation better.

Winnie looked to colleagues, parents, and school leaders to help her contend with this difficulty. Her search for support and assistance led to further frustration. She recalls her attempts to find help:

> It took me a few months, maybe two, to seek out help. I resisted confiding in administrators because I didn't want my gender to be an issue. I was concerned they would see this situation as a weakness of mine, not the school's or the boys'.

Even if the people who had hired Winnie encouraged her to come to them when she needed help, she retained the impression that any calls for help would be perceived as an admission of fault on her part. In time, however, she sought some support:

> Eventually, I confided in another female teacher and a male teacher/football coach. She offered commiseration, and he often would walk down the hall with me whenever we had similar schedules. The dean of students told me, "Well, boys will be boys. After all, you're all they've got to look at."

She notes this response from a parent: "Once a father of one of my students said to me, 'Oh well, I see how Tom has a hard time concentrating, now that I see you.'" The consistent response was a validation of the boys' attitude; it was embedded in the school culture. Winnie was left with the impression that it would be futile to try to change the boys or to equip herself with a strategy for contending with the behaviors she found disturbing.

When it was clear that others were not going to intercede on her behalf, Winnie took matters into her own hands.

> I started to confront some of the boys directly about their behavior or attitudes. It was a difficult task since I often didn't see who was whistling or making comments. I recall walking up to one group and asking, "Who is whistling at me?" They all looked sheepish and no one responded. I then told them it was wrong to whistle at a teacher that way and that I was disgusted, not flattered. My attitude also changed as I learned to accept that it wasn't my problem, it was theirs.

Any change required Winnie to take action herself by addressing the boys directly. To be able to confront the boys, she first had to deny the prevailing attitude that "Boys will be boys" and acknowledge that the problem lay with the boys and not with her being young, female, and attractive. In a sense, she had to convince herself that she was not at fault for being who she was.

Winnie makes it clear that the problems occurred outside of her regular classroom environment, with students who were not from her classes and with whom she was not acquainted. It appears that when she was in the classroom with students she knew, with her teacher persona established, and with a rapport already developed, Winnie had a more positive experience. It was in the relatively unstructured climate of the hallways, where some students could retain anonymity and assume roles that were distinct from their role in the classroom, that Winnie felt most stressed and vulnerable. Her school experience, then, was defined by factors that went beyond how well she was doing in planning engaging lessons and managing students in the classroom. Several factors—the school culture, the parents' attitudes, the lack of support from school leaders—combined with Winnie's personal characteristics to determine the nature of her first-year experience.

Christy's Case

For her first year, Christy taught in a predominantly white high school in an affluent community. Christy herself is African American. This is the way she describes the setting:

> Last year I taught in a very affluent high school . . . very high in socioeconomic status. Most of the students were [children of] CEOs or of that nature. . . . This was a public school. These kids come from well-off families. I say that because . . . when dealing with these types of children, if anything went wrong a parent would respond, "Well, did you see my kid do such and such?"

Christy had anticipated that the parents might be aggressive in advocating for their children. Christy also anticipated that she could rely on the support of her department chair, who was the only other African American on the faculty.

Christy's experience with a series of frustrations began when she took her class outside of the building on a warm day. They sat on the lawn near a lagoon and read *Romeo and Juliet*. When the class attempted to return to the building, Christy discovered that they were locked out of the entrance from which they had exited. While the class waited for someone to open the door, two boys who had long been adversaries began to scuffle. They threw some punches before Christy broke up the fight. By this time, an assistant principal was at the door and witnessed the brief fight between the two boys.

For Christy, the difficulty occurred when the students were suspended and a parent of one of the boys directed criticism at the teacher.

> The following day, there was a photocopy letter in my mailbox. It wasn't addressed to me. It was a photocopy addressed to the dean from this boy's father who blasted my reasoning, my thoughts for becoming a teacher, told me that I was influencing young minds, and I need to rethink my career choice and just blasted my integrity as a teacher.

Although it was disturbing to face the criticism of a parent, Christy felt confident that she could rely on the support of her department chair. She judged that it would be best to share the letter with him so that he would be aware of any parent concerns.

> I went and I told my department chair, who said, "Oh, don't worry about it. We'll take care of it, no problem." I let him read the letter, and I felt real good because up until this time we had always had a good relationship. He said, "We're going to have a meeting with the vice principal and we'll fix it."

When the subsequent meeting occurred, Christy did not receive the support she had expected. Instead, she felt attacked and betrayed.

> When we get into the meeting with my department chair and one of the vice principals . . . [and] closed the door, . . . they proceeded to talk about the incident plus every other mistake I had made as a new teacher . . . EVERYTHING! . . . They apparently had been documenting everything and they resurfaced *everything*. . . . They were so gentle in tone and so politically correct in their verbiage. . . . I was still very, very angry. I felt very betrayed because up until this point, it was all . . . everything is harmony . . . everything is wonderful. . . . Not only had I been ripped up by this parent indirectly, now I have my two superiors doing the same thing.

Christy had believed that any correctives that supervisors had recommended for improving her performance were no longer issues once she had corrected the problems. She had not expected there to be a cumulative effect from earlier observations and discussions of her shortcomings. She also judged that her supervisors were now finding fault with her when she had not done anything wrong. She was especially disappointed that her department chair did not support her. She notes, "He was also of the same ethnicity as me, and we were the only two in the entire school. I didn't trust him at all [from then on] because it went from this identity of same culture to something . . . total surprise." She had thought that she and her department chair had a positive rapport, a shared experience, and an unstated bond. When she experienced what she considered a betrayal, she distanced herself from her department chair and from administrators in the school.

> At that point as a new teacher, I was afraid of administration. I was thinking that this was going to go on my permanent record. I was up for an evaluation soon. I was like, "Oh, my God, they are going to fire me." None of which they did. . . . It never came up again. . . . I never heard from the parent. I never heard what steps were taken . . . *nothing*! At the end of the year, I quit.

The balance of the year was uneasy for Christy because she felt she could not perform as the person she imagined herself to be: "I couldn't really be *me* anymore because my first thought was to stay out of trouble and not to cause any more ruckus. It definitely took away from my teaching style." Although there were no similar episodes for Christy, the experience tainted everything about the job for the rest of the year: "I still got a nice evaluation. There was no follow-up, so for a while I walked on eggshells because I thought it was going to come back up, but it never did. It never came back up."

In her reflection on the episode, Christy notes that the uniqueness of her situation at the school contributed significantly to the long-term effects:

> The distrust afterward definitely was a race thing. We were the only two there. I had that understood trust, most definitely . . . but after that situation, I still talked to him; he was still a very good source of information. He still told me the right thing to do. He was still a very wonderful department chair, but the personal trust was gone. As far as administration, I don't tell them everything. They're administration. I didn't have any personal relationship with the administration.

Several factors combined to affect Christy's initial experience in teaching. A problem that began as an isolated classroom management issue extended into a conflict with a parent, which in turn evolved into erosion of trust in supervisors of the current job and in those in the future. As was the case with Winnie, a dynamic complex of interactive factors defined this teacher's first-year experience. Although we can generalize about the experiences and concerns of beginning teachers, we must also realize that the factors unique to the person, to the assignment, and to the school setting will combine to present both joys and frustrations.

The experiences of all the new teachers in this study illustrate the potential difficulty that inexperienced teachers are likely to have in entering a school where the students represent a variety of cultures that are largely unfamiliar to the newcomers. Johnson (2004) summarizes the increasingly common challenge:

> [T]he students—their behavior, their skills, and their needs—can be the most surprising part of teaching for new teachers. This is particularly true for those who have been out of school themselves for a long time, or who are teaching in schools outside of the communities most familiar to them. (p. 74)

The contrasts can take many forms. Obvious contrasts will be like those Winnie and Christy experienced—based on differences in gender, culture, or ethnicity. Less obvious contrasts might include the new teacher, who has often been academically successful and enthusiastic about school, meeting in the first teaching assignment a group of students who struggle and hate school. In all cases, the new teacher will have to develop ways to contend with the unfamiliarity. As we discuss in Chapter 9, it is the clear responsibility of universities and schools to prepare new teachers to work successfully in an unfamiliar environment, and in that chapter we suggest some modest steps that preparation and inservice training can take.

Coping Strategies

One can imagine the negative effect on a teacher's health when a relentless pageant of obligations consumes most of his or her waking hours. The picture that beginning teachers report appears a bleak one, with long hours, some episodes of disrespect and disorder, and lack of support. An objective observer would have to wonder how these teachers survive and why they continue to do what they do. Another pattern among the interviews sheds some light on endurance and growth.

First, teachers manage to cope because they hold on to the belief that ultimately things will get better. They have a realistic projection that they will find a way to correct or improve situations that are the source or irritation, frustration, and anxiety. In the interviews, teachers identify an important element in their coping strategies as simply enduring difficulties until the situation improves. Here is what Gordon says about managing the stress of an exhausting workload:

> I think I went through some mild depression for a little bit, but I realized what it was because I was killing myself with these hours. I'm not getting out and I'm not seeing the sun all day. I recognized that and said, "It will be over soon." The second year will be better and the third year will probably be better than that. I guess my plans are to bite the bullet for the first year and second year, too, and push through it.

Gordon is not a glutton for punishment. He does not plan to continue his career in the same way he worked his first year. He has learned from experience and realistically expects that the hours will be fewer and the activities in his life will be more balanced. He is confident that he has a strategy that works for him:

> I think essentially that the way I'm looking at it has helped me get through to know there is a light at the end of the tunnel. . . . Things will get better and it's reasonable to expect to do a ton of work, especially at the very beginning; then you learn to manage that a little bit of what you need to do and what you really don't need to do in your preparation. Think about the entire year that way. Going into it, I thought about the entire year being a ton of work at the beginning that would taper off just a little bit.

We would have to wonder about the wisdom of sending into a classroom every day a teacher who feels that the situation is bad and will never get better. The beginning teachers report that a teacher has to have a sense of hope and tenacity. Clara, a student teacher, reports this experience:

> I remember I would go home and I would tell myself that "you're only doing this for a couple of weeks. Do the best that you can. Don't be too hard on yourself. Just try to do the best you can." I started experimenting and tried different types of strategies to get [students] to behave. I started using different types of activities: things that they might be more engaged in, things that might

interest them. It took a long time because the things I thought would work, didn't work.

But Clara endured until, as she describes,

> Once I got adjusted, they adjusted to me. I started doing things differently. I seemed to encounter some kind of hurdle, and once I got past all of this it has been completely better ever since I got over this hurdle essentially with them. . . . It is just totally different.

Clara emphasizes, however, that she did not just passively accept abuse or ignore reprehensible behavior:

> It was kind of like I just thought, "I need to stick it out. It's probably going to be unpleasant for a while, but that's how I have to deal with it, how they should learn to deal it." It wasn't like a passive endurance. During this whole time, I was working my butt off trying [as] many different things as I could. I was racking my brain at night: What can I do better tomorrow? Is it my lesson? Is it my behavior? I was constantly thinking of things.

A sense of hope that things will get better apparently supports the teacher's endurance; but at the same time, the teacher is consciously working strategically to make things better.

The good news in the bleak reports is that over time things got better for the teachers. They report that along with the fatigue and frustrations they experienced fun lessons, developed strong personal relationships, and witnessed growth in student learning.

Follow-up

Interviews

We conducted follow-up interviews with six of the original eleven novice teachers. Only six of the original eleven subjects were available for us to interview again. (See Appendix D for the follow-up interview questions and protocol.) Two of the six are no longer teaching. The two who have left teaching are perhaps the two most invested in teaching, but circumstances have influenced them to leave the profession for now, with the hope that they will return to teaching at some point in the future.

We collected the follow-up interviews to track the teachers' changes over a year and to look for patterns that might indicate which teachers were vulnerable to leaving the profession before reaching tenure. We also wanted to identify the factors that influenced teachers to continue in teaching. A summary of the patterns of speech among the six interviewees' responses appears in Table 4.1. The following discussion is in two parts: (1) the comments of those teachers who are *unlikely* to stay in the profession beyond the first five years, and (2) the comments of those teachers who are *likely* to stay in the profession beyond the first five years.

Those Who Are Unlikely to Stay

First, those teachers who seem unlikely to persevere in teaching talk about how the workload is unreasonable and hopeless. Drew observes, "This year I came home and I have so much work to do. I don't know how to fix that. Veteran teachers all say that they don't have an answer. None of them felt that they did it well." Drew sees the problem of a burdensome workload as inherent in teaching, especially in the teaching of English. He complains, "If I taught another subject, it would be easier. In English there is so much to think about and worry about, and so much to grade." Christy also identifies the workload as one of the most difficult aspects of her job: "Being an English teacher, I don't like all the work I have to take home. I still want a life. Even if I had thirty kids, as long as I didn't have as much to take home, that would be better." For both Drew and Christy, the time-consuming burden of grading papers night after night and planning lessons is one of the worst aspects of the job. They do not see much potential for the situation to get better. They note that the diffi-

TABLE **4.1.** Patterns of Speech among Beginning Teachers:
Those Who Are Likely to Stay and Those Who Are Likely to Leave

---

Those Who Are Likely to Leave after a Relatively Short Time:

- ◆ Talk about how the workload is unreasonable and hopeless
- ◆ Talk about the futility of any efforts to correct the problems they see as inherent to teaching
- ◆ Talk more about their needs than the needs of the students
- ◆ Talk about their plans to "escape" from teaching
- ◆ Talk about their limited career choices and their view of teaching as a career compromise

Those Who Are Likely to Stay in Teaching:

- ◆ Talk about a sense of duty to help the young people who can benefit from the teacher's instruction
- ◆ Talk about an interest in developing their teaching skills
- ◆ Talk about their growth as teachers and can account for factors that have influenced their growth
- ◆ Talk about strategic plans to make bad situations better
- ◆ Talk about bad experiences in the school as evidence of the need for good teachers
- ◆ Talk about disturbing episodes in the school year as shared experiences between students and faculty and not as personal obstacles, aggravations, or attacks.

culty could be corrected if their teaching load changed significantly or if they were to teach a different subject, neither of which they see as a realistic possibility. They recognize that the ponderous paper grading responsibility is inherent in teaching English and will never diminish. Drew notes that he has asked veteran teachers how to "fix" the problem, but no one has a solution. For Drew and Christy, the paper load remains a hopeless problem.

It appears that those teachers who are likely to leave the profession early are those who talk more about their own needs than the needs of the students. Drew reports that he recently married, and he is more inclined to spend time with his wife doing such things as watching television and taking walks and less inclined to spend a lot of time on school work: "I spend more time with my wife and less time on the paperwork." He is a competitive runner and reports, "I still am an enthusiastic runner. My commitment to running does require some of my time as well. If you are going to run, there is not a lot of room for compromise." Nadine expresses her current disappointment that her teaching experience was not what she had imagined it would be: "My reality as a teacher is so much different than my reasons for entering the profession. I love studying literature, but the English skills that I attempt to teach are often put on the backburner." She also reports her frustration in working with teenagers: "I don't think that I can work with teenagers for the rest of my life. I have a very difficult time dealing with student apathy, and I don't think I am equipped to deal with it for much longer, nor do I want to." These are candid reflections on their current teaching situations; but if these teachers are to survive much longer in the profession, they will need the support or understanding that allows them to balance personal needs and job demands, and they will need to find something valuable and compelling in what they do.

Perhaps the most revealing indicator that a teacher will leave the profession before earning tenure is his or her explicit expression of plans for exiting the job. Nadine shares this scenario:

> I will probably stay in teaching for just a few more years. . . . I
> have a feeling that I will quickly get stuck in a rut, and I think

that when I have an "epiphany" about what I would like to do next, I will not feel too bad about jumping at the opportunity.

Drew lays out the specific timetable:

> I got married this year. We do want to have a family. My wife makes a decent salary. One of us will stay home with the kids. I would like to be the one. The plan is for me to stay home. I would leave to raise kids.

After three years of teaching, Christy plans to stay in education, but she wants to leave the classroom: "I do plan to teach for a few more years; but at my earliest opportunity to get out of the classroom, I will and get into administration." These three teachers report that they are on a clear path toward departure from the classroom and, in two instances, departure from education altogether. A supervisor or mentor would be hard-pressed to find the morale-boosting words that would inspire these teachers to invest their futures in teaching and stay in the profession beyond the initial years.

Part of the teachers' willingness to leave teaching derives from their sense that for them teaching was a compromise career when other paths did not seem clear or attainable. Christy talks about the relative security in teaching: "I do see myself outside of the classroom, but I'm not prepared yet. In our economy, I feel safe in my profession." Nadine concludes more than once that teaching is a compromise for her and she would like to explore other options. She notes, "I do like my job, but to some extent, I have stayed in teaching because I do not know what else I want to do." She has imagined the prospect of leaving teaching:

> I realize that I might not be able to make what I am currently making if I were to get an entry-level job elsewhere. At the beginning of this year, I seriously thought about leaving the profession, but with the events and aftermath of 9/11, I decided that my job security was more important than my job satisfaction.

The expressions of discontent, the recognition of teaching as a compromise career choice, and the statement of plans for exiting the profession seem to add up to a profile of someone who will not stay in teaching until reaching tenure and developing into a skilled teacher.

The especially discouraging aspect of the teachers' inclinations to leave is that by all accounts they are good teachers who show every promise of developing into highly skilled teachers. Their supervisors appreciate their work, and their students speak highly of them as teachers. Again, for the supervisor or mentor who recognizes the signs of departure, it would be difficult to know how to intervene, or even to decide whether to intervene. We fear that in some instances, a supervisor who recognizes that a teacher is determined to leave may reduce the extent of the effort to support and develop that teacher.

Those Who Are Likely to Stay

Perhaps the first indicator that a teacher is likely to stay in the profession for many years is that he or she talks about a sense of duty to help the young people who can benefit from the teacher's instruction. Nora explains her motivation for teaching:

> I think that there is such a need for good people, it's incredible. In some sense it is a fear that if I'm not here, who will take care of the kids? I have reason to get up in the morning. I know kids have liked English for the first time. . . . I know for some students, I have literally saved their lives.

For Nora the commitment to teaching is an altruistic resolution that goes well beyond sharing the concepts and skills of a subject. For Gordon the holistic experience of being a teacher satisfies his altruistic, intellectual, and spiritual inclinations:

> Being a teacher really "took" with me. It became part of who I am. It is *natural* and *organic*. Having the right experiences as a teacher is an influence, having appropriate support and guidance in finding ways for the practice to be natural.

In Gordon's case, he was "naturally" inclined to be a teacher, and the environment in which he worked supported his inclinations and did nothing to discourage his development as a professional.

Although Brendan left teaching because of personal pressures, he still speaks of a sense of mission:

> When I was teaching, I truly felt important. I felt that everything I did would impact the lives of my students. I felt like I was contributing to the continued development of our local and national communities. I used to say to somebody, anybody, at least once or twice a week, that I have the greatest job there is.

These teachers recognize that there are challenges in schools—troubled homes, dangerous neighborhoods, poor skills, strained resources—but the teachers who stay in the profession do not see the challenges as excuses for leaving; instead, they recognize the difficulties as compelling evidence that they need to be in the schools.

Nora, Gordon, and Brendan talk about an interest in developing their teaching skills, and they can account for factors that have influenced their growth. Nora notes that much of her influence on her students has been "gratifying, but scary too." She reports that while she has changed the lives of some students, "I also know that there are a lot of students I haven't reached yet, so I have to get better." She describes the need to grow in order to influence her students' growth. Gordon describes a reciprocal effect as he and the students develop together:

> It was important to find things that were important to me and to the students. When you are working in the spirit of inquiry, it makes it an authentic experience for me. I was influenced to read more and think about the authentic questions. In the process, I became a better teacher. There was support from the department chair, the principal, and colleagues. There was academic and affective support.

The students influenced both Nora and Gordon to grow, but the intellectual environment of their schools also made development possible as colleagues and supervisors contributed to the intellectual life of the beginning teachers and supported their development. Brendan, who has left teaching, summarizes the satisfaction he found unique to teaching: "Teaching was fulfilling for me. I felt that I was constantly growing, learning, and sharing. Most of that has changed now, however."

The survivors also talk about strategic plans to make bad situations better. In his initial interview, for example, Gordon described the stress of an overwhelming workload, but at the time he forecast that his management of time would improve, and he worked toward that improvement:

> We had discussed the amount of time involved in teaching. I expected things would get better, and they have gotten better. I can plan in a more economical way and have room for being creative. Now I have time to do a lot of other reading that ultimately influences my way of teaching and thinking about education.

Nora faces a similar workload challenge:

> I have to take care of myself physically. My day goes from 5 a.m. to 9 p.m. when I'm coaching. This year, I coached basketball and softball, so I've been coaching since November. Sometimes, I am too tired to eat dinner. I have to reduce the workload.

While the workload is now overwhelming, Nora does not give up hope; instead, she sees a problem that needs correcting, one that she realistically senses is correctable.

For the teachers who are likely to continue, the beginning stage of their teaching careers has not been all positive. They have faced a variety of stresses and some nightmarish sorrows. But they talk about disturbing episodes in the school year as shared experiences between students and faculty and not as personal obstacles, aggravations, or attacks. Nora, for example, observes,

> I've had some really spectacular moments. . . . This year has been intense. One of my students died of an overdose. The policy here is not to report when someone has died. I had to break it to my students that one of their classmates died of a drug overdose. There was no counseling or support for the students in the building. Students are still hurting, seeing a fifteen-year-old in a coffin. They were clinging to me for help. It was tough to come back into the classroom. It brought us together for emotional support.

Obviously, for Nora and her students the death of a classmate was a staggering loss, representing a time in Nora's first year of teaching when she might have doubted that she could endure the profession. She speaks, however, of the obligation to provide the strength and emotional support to help her students endure. When Nora concludes that the experience of realizing the death of a fifteen-year-old student forced her students to cling to her and to one another, she verifies her impression that the students need her and that she serves a crucial function. At the same time, Nora reports, her first year of teaching has changed her significantly. She reflects on the impact of her first year of teaching:

> I have become a darker person. I'm idealistic at heart, but things that I've seen daily have made me laugh less and lose some of my youth. I have become more callous, and I see it more when I interact with people who are not teachers. It seems that their hearts are not as heavy.

Although Nora reports the negative effect the first year of teaching has had on her, she reveals a resolve to grow, to make changes, and to continue to serve her students.

A Caution

We have realistic recollections of our own limitations and shaky confidence when we each began teaching. We know we experienced many moments of doubt: those we expressed openly and those we kept closely guarded. We want to caution here against making the abrupt and hasty judgment that because a preservice or beginning teacher shows inclinations toward leaving the profession, it is preordained that the teacher *must* or *will* leave the profession. In most cases, we are hesitant to presume to know that an aspiring teacher will never make it as a teacher. Some indicators are obvious. We recall, for example, one preservice teacher who smelled conspicuously of strong drink whenever we encountered him and spoke furtively of a conspiracy among Serbian assassins and IRA operatives to execute him. We judged with some assurance that under his current state of mind he was not prepared to take independent charge of groups of children.

   When we recognize patterns of speech that suggest a teacher

is *likely* to leave the profession, we do not see this as an opportunity to counsel that person away from teaching. Instead, we recommend searching for the sources of discontent and the obstacles to making the job a rewarding and fulfilling one, and working with the teacher to reduce the obstacles and elevate the rewards. In short, we see the task ahead as one of helping the new teacher to redirect himself or herself to the goals and motivations that brought the teacher to the profession in the first place, rather than hastily showing the teacher the door.

Some Advice from New Teachers

The beginning teachers we interviewed offer some advice for teacher preparation programs and for schools. Gordon encourages teachers to have a firm theoretical foundation to guide pedagogy:

> It helps to have a theoretical basis to guide planning and purpose. Having a theoretical model allows someone to be reflective and have a chance to be satisfied. The alternative would be to manage classroom activities that really have little meaning. Theory is not an unnatural construct, but finding a natural connection.

Brendan sees value in immersing the preservice teacher in the realities of teaching for an extended period of time: "Student teaching should be a minimum of sixteen weeks in order to provide an accurate sense of what a semester is like. Luckily, my student teaching experience was that long, but I know others are not." The theoretical framework drives the planning and supports reflection. The extended practice provides the experience to validate theory and fix belief.

Many schools point with pride to the mentoring program that senior staff have designed to support the induction of new teachers. Nora cautions us, however, that it is the *quality* of the mentoring program that will make all the difference. Nora regrets her experience with a mentor:

> The mentoring program is such a sham. It is the most ridiculous thing I've ever been to. It would actually drive people out of

teaching. There are meetings on Friday nights from five to eight and we don't get paid for it. For example, they *read* to us out of the discipline code. My mentor did not want to be a mentor. She hates me; I hate her. I wanted to be with another teacher with whom I have more in common, and a *good* teacher.

Nora points to some obvious problems with some mentoring programs: If the time required to participate in the program represents an additional burden on the beginning teacher, the activities become counterproductive. Novices will naturally select mentors they respect and trust. When mentors are randomly or capriciously assigned to new teachers, the novices will resist and resent the mentor program. New teachers can help to identify their needs during the trying times of pretenure experience. Research on the concerns of beginning teachers can also guide the activities of mentoring programs. Nora reports that required, burdensome, and perfunctory mentoring programs are likely to discourage the novice.

Gordon, who reports commonly putting in fourteen-hour days during his first year of teaching, offers this insight:

> During the first year, the workload took me away from friends, which leads to some depression. Beginning teachers may need some kind of counseling, and [to] engage in conversations, which might ease depression. Having an opportunity for personal connections can make the experience more pleasant.

Again, as Lortie (1977) points out, teaching can be an isolating experience. This is especially true in the first year of an individual's career when the environment is new and everyone in the school is a stranger. While mentoring programs connect the inexperienced teacher with an older and more experienced teacher, Gordon reminds us that personal connections of all sorts will help the new teacher to develop and thrive. In some instances, a variety of formal and informal mentor relationships will be helpful, but it is also crucial that the novice have frequent contact with peers, who can seem less threatening and more empathic.

Survey Results

Survey of Attitudes

An analysis of the interviews with novice teachers suggests that a common source of concern and frustration is the radical mismatch between the expectations that beginning teachers had for teaching before they began teaching, and the actual experience of teaching when they began their careers. We posed this question: Do preservice teachers have significant misconceptions about the nature of the job of teaching?

Teachers in training at six different universities from different regions of the country and experienced English teachers at six different high schools completed surveys to help us explore this issue. The Teacher Expectation Survey and the Teacher Experience Survey appear as Appendixes B and C, respectively. A total of 218 preservice teachers responded to the Teacher Expectation Survey. English department faculty members at six public high schools in the Midwest responded to the Teacher Experience Survey. One of the public schools was a small school in a rural area; five were large high schools in a variety of suburban communities, some affluent and some with large low-income populations. A total of 141 experienced teachers responded.

The survey data support conclusions suggested by the analysis of the interviews of novice teachers. Summaries of the survey results and findings appear in Tables 5.1 to 5.4. The surveys were constructed with items under nine categories, which were identified from the initial teacher interviews (see Table 3.1). Table 5.1 shows where novice teachers and experienced teachers differ significantly from each other. In response to only one category do the preservice teachers express more confidence in their abilities than the experienced teachers express in theirs (see Table 5.2).

The survey results reveal that preservice teachers do not have a realistic idea of the workload of a high school English teacher, the fatigue they might experience, or the negative effects the fatigue might have on their physical and emotional well-being.

A factor analysis[1] of the survey results supports the coherence of seven of the nine categories as being valid categories (Table 5.1). The seven categories supported by the factor analysis are Parents, Colleagues, Grading, Workload, Autonomy, Physical Characteristics, and Knowledge and Preparation. The analysis also produced an eighth category that combined a number of questions from what were considered different categories.

This eighth category consisted of questions 8, 9, 10, 16, 17, 18, 20, 21, 28, and 42 (see Appendixes B and C for the questions). Examining these questions indicates that perhaps a good name for the new category would be Classrooms, as all of the questions, regardless of which category the questions were originally drawn from, relate to activities in classrooms during teaching. Table 5.3 gives a summary of the factor analysis.

TABLE 5.1. Analysis of Variance for Teacher Attitudes

Source	Df	F	η^2	p	Power ($\alpha = .05$)
		Between subjects			
Students	1	5.631*	.023	.018	.657
Parents	1	.246	.001	.620	.078
Colleagues	1	2.579	.011	.110	.359
Supervisors	1	4.142*	.017	.043	.527
Grading	1	13.754***	.055	.000	.959
Workload	1	11.573**	.046	.001	.923
Autonomy	1	30.693***	.114	.000	1.000
Physical Characteristics	1	27.029***	.102	.000	.999
Knowledge & Preparation	1	6.062*	.025	.015	.689

*$p < .05$.
**$p < .01$.
***$p < .001$.

TABLE 5.2. Summary of Significant Findings Related to Teacher Attitudes

Practicing teachers are significantly more confident than preservice teachers:
◆ about experiencing a *positive relationship with supervisors*
◆ about experiencing a *positive relationship with students* (including *classroom management*)
◆ that their *preparation and content knowledge* are sufficient for their job
◆ about having *autonomy* in their own classrooms
◆ about *grading* and their ability to *assess students' performances*
◆ that *physical and other personal characteristics* will not impede their ability to do their jobs
Preservice teachers are significantly more confident than practicing teachers:
◆ that they *can handle the workload* and that it will not have a deleterious effect on physical health and emotional well-being
No significant differences were found between practicing teachers and preservice teachers:
◆ in experiencing a *positive relationship with supervisors**
◆ in experiencing a *postivite relationship with the parents* of their students*

* *Observed power* was too small to detect differences if they do exist.

TABLE 5.3. Analysis of Variance for Teacher Attitudes from Factor Analysis

Source	Df	F	η^2	p	Power ($\alpha= .05$)
		Between subjects			
Classrooms	1	1.703	.005	.193	.255
Parents	1	.275	.001	.600	.082
Colleagues	1	6.618**	.021	.009	.740
Grading	1	27.120***	.080	.000	.999
Workload	1	9.936**	.031	.193	.881
Autonomy	1	22.207***	.066	.000	.997
Physical Characteristics	1	25.022***	.074	.002	.999
Knowledge & Preparation	1	0.024	.000	.956	.050

*$p < .05$.
**$p < .01$.
***$p < .001$.

In examining Table 5.3, it is important to recall that factor analysis removes many questions from the analysis. Of the original sixty-seven questions, only forty-one are retained after the factor analysis. Hence, it is expected that both the power and the effect size (η^2) will decrease, and, in general, this is the case. Because of the lack of significance of the new category, it is difficult to use that category to reexamine the qualitative data; future research, however, should be aware of the possibility of this alternative interpretation.

Fatigue Factor

We find it to be both predictable and noteworthy that preservice teachers express more confidence than experienced teachers in their ability to handle the workload. Our years of working with beginning teachers confirm that they rarely have a realistic view of the workload involved in teaching, and especially in teaching high school English. In part, this might be a product of youth, when one enjoys strength, vigor, seemingly inexhaustible energy, and the optimistic assumption of invulnerability. At the same time, preservice teachers perceive their university workload as oppressively heavy, making it difficult to imagine that the load can increase. In addition, it is difficult to catch genuine glimpses of teachers at work in the multiple phases that constitute that work—planning, grading, writing, phoning, meeting, collaborating. As a student, one might get the impression that teachers work with ease and comfort, coming into a room, demanding attention, and talking effortlessly about topics familiar to them. Of course, popular media never portray the daily grind of teaching, just the leisurely glibness of a Mr. Kotter in *"Welcome Back, Kotter,"* or the pathetic perfunctory routine of Ben Stein in *Ferris Bueller's Day Off*. Even when teachers are portrayed as gifted and inspiring, as do Robin Williams in *Dead Poets Society* and Michelle Pfeiffer in *Dangerous Minds*, they appear to achieve their effect on students through strength of personality and obvious compassion, not through daily careful preparation and strategic planning.

We recognize that having a realistic sense of the task of teaching can vary widely by subject area and by length and nature of the field experience that is part of the teacher training program. Some of our university colleagues who train elementary teachers, who spend much time in classrooms in schools over the course of two years, report that novice elementary school teachers are bound to have a better sense than their secondary school counterparts of the work involved in teaching. It is common for students training to become English teachers to spend less than a full semester working in a high school. The student teaching experience in itself does not fully reveal the daunting nature of the work of teaching because most apprentice teachers operate with a limited load of classes under the careful guidance of a cooperating teacher and a university supervisor. The genuine experience occurs only when the new teacher is operating independently, with a full load of classes and less support from attentive mentors.

A crucial revelation is the implication that most high school English teachers come into the profession with a less than realistic picture of the workload they will experience. Our interviews with beginning teachers help to round out the picture suggested by the survey data. Typically, most new teachers are hired in the late spring or early summer. Equipped with knowledge about their teaching assignment, and with most of the summer to prepare, the new teacher can begin the school year with weeks' worth of plans, even if only in outline form. It is also typical for new teachers to have a relatively easy time managing students at the beginning of the year, when both the teacher and the students are getting to know each other and students are still intent on beginning the school year in the most positive way possible. We find, then, that a very vulnerable time for new teachers is the end of October, when an array of factors combine to wear the new teachers down. We say more about this critical time in Chapter 6.

Here is what new English teachers tell us: A few weeks into the school year, they begin to run out of the lessons they prepared during the summer. This means that each night teachers go home and attempt to devise new lessons, and new teachers have no file of previously attempted lessons to support and guide preparation. At the same time, of course, teachers are contending with stacks of papers and tests collected from scores of students. New teachers might also find that exposure to a building of students with a variety of viruses and infections has caused them to suffer at least a cold or other low-grade infection. One of our interviewees noted that after a few weeks into the school year, the "honeymoon period with the students was over," and many tested her ability to manage the class. Then the end of the first grading period requires that new English teachers complete all the grading and calculate weeks' worth of papers and tests in order to submit summary grades for all students. To further complicate matters, new teachers might have coaching, club, or committee responsibilities. It's not hard to imagine the sick, harried, and stressed teachers at the end of October feeling a fatigue unlike any weariness they have ever experienced. When new teachers study a relatively paltry paycheck under these circumstances, it is understandable that they might consider that the intangible emotional and intellectual rewards of teaching and the tangible yet modest monetary rewards do not begin to compensate for the debilitating stress and fatigue of the job. Exit surveys of teachers who leave the profession indicate that many teachers leave because of "poor pay" (Wayne, 2000). Of course, "poor pay" is a concept relative to the nature of the task for which one is compensated. If the job is easy and pleasant, a modest salary would seem fair; but if the job is stressful and increasingly taxing, a modest salary begins to look inequitable.

As we discuss at greater length in a later chapter, it is critical that universities and schools anticipate that the fatigue factor will be a crucial one. For the universities, it will be important to structure substantial time for preservice teachers to work in schools and do more than observe. They must be involved often and for a substantial length of time in doing teacher tasks in schools. Once someone begins teaching, the school must ensure that a supervisor and mentors are sensitive to the patterns of work, stress, and fatigue and can anticipate the vulnerable episodes in the beginning stages of the teacher's experience. In a sense, no one can fully explain the fatigue and paint an absolutely accurate picture of the challenges of the job; but supervisors, mentors, and peers can help new teachers manage some aspects of the job and reassure them that the sense of being over-whelmed is normal and that there are means and hope for mak-ing matters better.

On Becoming a Teacher

The survey results also reveal that preservice teachers harbor sig-nificant doubts about who they will be as teachers and how they will be accepted by students and supervisors. The new teachers begin the profession with doubts about their knowledge and preparation for completing their teaching assignment. They are also less confident than the experienced teachers about how they will grade their students' work and how much autonomy they will have in their own classrooms.

The survey data support the picture of becoming a teacher that the interviews suggest. In short, the experienced teachers know who they are. They are not particularly troubled or anx-ious about their relationships with students, parents, or supervi-sors. In fact, experienced teachers appear to make little distinction between their supervisors and other colleagues. The veteran teach-ers express confidence that they have a positive rapport with their students and can skillfully manage classes. They indicate that they have the knowledge necessary to teach whatever they are assigned to teach, and they have the autonomy to teach the way they feel comfortable teaching. The experienced teachers cannot imagine that any personal or physical characteristics will inter-fere with their ability to do their job.

The attitudes expressed by the experienced teachers are those that come with age and experience, factors that cannot be built into any teacher preparation or inservice program. The experi-enced teachers are confident in who they are and in the notion that they can do what needs to be done from year to year, with new students and with new teaching situations. In contrast, be-ginning teachers are in the process of growing into their roles. New teachers wonder if what they are doing—in designing les-sons, responding to students, interacting with parents—is what bona fide teachers do. Imagine a teaching scenario in which the students are a bit talkative while the teacher is giving directions.

Among other concerns, the new teacher wonders when it is time to pause to correct someone. And if it is time to intervene, does the teacher single out a particular student or correct the entire class, guilty and innocent alike? The teacher wonders from day to day if he or she is being too lenient or too tough. Young teachers want to take advantage of their youthful appeal in forming positive relationships with students; they do not, after all, want to appear to be like the grumpy, middle-aged veterans that some students complain about. At the same time, teachers, young or old, inevitably remain apart from the lives and experience of current adolescents. To complicate matters, new teachers, not far themselves from adolescent self-consciousness, may wonder if such characteristics as gender, height, weight, or ethnicity will inhibit their ability to do the job. The challenge is a balancing act, and new teachers look to models far and near to figure out how to act the part of a teacher.

In their worries about their preparation and knowledge for teaching their subject, new teachers might have in mind that the veteran teachers, like their college professors, are subject specialists, with a scholarly command of some area of literature or language. While the person preparing at college to become an English teacher will be studying Shakespeare and Milton and Spencer, there is a very good chance that as a new teacher this same person will encounter groups of lower-ability students who are required to read *The Outsiders* or similar young adult literature and to answer study guide questions. The literature may be something foreign and undervalued by the new teacher, and yet he or she must share it in a meaningful way with students who are reluctant to read anything the school sponsors as worthy of reading. Little wonder if the new English teacher has some doubts about his or her preparation and knowledge for teaching what is required. And if the new teacher decides that the literature and other material that someone else has designated as essential for a particular group of students isn't worthy of serious scholarship, does the novice have any recourse to make changes?

Veteran teachers would testify that many conflicts that develop with students and their parents derive from misunderstandings about grades. The survey data reveal that experienced teachers are significantly more confident than the new teachers that they have a fairly easy facility for assessing their students' work and determining grades. Over the years, veteran teachers have experienced a number of situations in which they have struggled to make the best choice about grades and had to negotiate systems for assessing and reporting grades in a reasonable way to students and parents. While everyone submits grades, the systems teachers use for determining, recording, and reporting grades may vary widely. It is understandable that new English teachers might feel less than confident when practices for assessment might not be standard and may at times seem whimsical. Also, assigning grades is a sensitive matter. Grades are value-laden and emotionally charged. For the new teacher who is trying to develop positive relationships with students and their parents but who feels an obligation to maintain some imagined standard and to protect an academic citadel, there will certainly be some doubts. In short, the new teacher wonders, what do real teachers do when faced with tough assessment situations?

Not One Size for All

Schools often try to support new teachers in their development through mentoring. In many mentoring situations, all new English teachers are treated as being the same. A cluster analysis[2] of the survey results, however, does not support this view of new teachers, identifying five primary groups of new teachers and three primary groups of experienced teachers. The clusters were determined using the original survey categories. It should be noted that although demographic data (e.g., age, gender, ethnicity) were not used in determining the clusters, there are differences between the clusters with regard to demographics.

Table 5.4 summarizes the primary characteristics of the clusters identified by the analysis for both new and experienced teachers. Only the cluster characteristics that are statistically significantly different from other clusters are given. Several features of the table are worth noting.

First, the characteristics given in Table 5.4 merely compare the clusters to one another. They do not necessarily indicate which factors are the most important to the development of a new teacher. Even though, for example, the grading category is not a difference between any of the clusters, this does not mean that professional development regarding grading is not an important need.

Second, note that three of the clusters of new teachers correspond closely to the three clusters of experienced teachers. It is tempting to draw the conclusion that those three clusters of novice teachers are the teachers who will stay and become experienced teachers. Such a conclusion, however, is not supported by

TABLE 5.4. Clusters of New and Experienced Teachers

New teachers	
Cluster	Primary characteristics
Cluster 1	These teachers are significantly more concerned about all areas of the survey than are the other clusters of new or experienced teachers.
Cluster 2	These teachers are significantly more concerned primarily about relationships with students and with supervisors than are the other new teacher clusters. This cluster also has a larger percentage of minority teachers than other clusters.
Cluster 3	These teachers are more concerned about workload than are teachers in any other category, and they are significantly more concerned about workload than are those in New Teacher Cluster 4. They are also mostly female.
Cluster 4	These teachers are more concerned about workload than are teachers in any other category. They differ from Cluster 3 because they are mostly male and are less concerned about workload than are those in New Teacher Cluster 3.
Cluster 5	These teachers are most concerned with their physical appearance. There does not seem to be a gender or ethnicity trend to this group.
Experienced teachers	
Cluster 1	These teachers are significantly more concerned about all areas of the survey than are other experienced teachers.
Cluster 2	These teachers are significantly more concerned primarily about relationships with students and with supervisors than are other groups of experienced teachers.
Cluster 3	These experienced teachers are more concerned about workload than are either of the other clusters of experienced teachers.

the data; it would require some form of longitudinal study to support such a conclusion.

Third, there is some possibility, as yet unexplored, that results from an instrument such as the current survey could be used to help identify appropriate mentoring topics for new teachers. This issue will be discussed in more depth in a later chapter. Such a discussion, however, is clouded a bit by the first point: we do not know if the new teachers' most pressing concerns are those that separate them from other groups.

Fourth, note that not all experienced teachers are the same. In discussions of teachers, there is often the implicit assumption that all good teachers are alike. While no one would attempt to defend that position, it is useful to be reminded of our need to see teachers as different from one another, even though there are similarities between teachers and though many experienced teachers have similar issues regarding their teaching.

Notes

1. Factor analysis is a technique that analyzes the interrelations between questions. It attempts to group the questions into a manageable number of meaningful categories.
2. A cluster analysis groups the respondents of a survey into a manageable number of groups. Each group is formed by those respondents who, based on their survey responses, are more like their group members than they are like respondents who are in other groups.

The Common Life of the First-Year Teacher

Preparing for the Unknown

Our work with student teachers and first-year teachers confirms that for most people, beginning a career in teaching is very stressful. The sad statistic that nearly one in three teachers who begin the profession leaves within the first three years confirms that becoming a teacher is difficult. We also know that those teachers who follow a "fast track" system of teacher preparation leave the profession in far greater numbers than those who follow a more extended and conventional teacher preparation program (Darling-Hammond & Youngs, 2002). Our surveys of preservice and practicing teachers suggest also that many beginners enter the profession with inaccurate and unrealistic expectations about their approaching experience. Obviously, programs for preparing teachers in a way that will encourage retention are complex, attending to such factors as subject area knowledge, pedagogy, field experience, and practice teaching. We judge that it would be helpful for teachers entering their first year of teaching to study a projection of the common experience of a first-year teacher.

We emphasize that building into teacher preparation programs an awareness of the reality of the teaching experience is just one of many components of teacher preparation, but it is a critical consideration. A medical analogy will suggest the importance of making prospective teachers aware of the pattern of experience they are likely to encounter during the first year of teaching. Medical professionals understand that a patient who faces major surgery will find the experience extremely stressful. No hospital staff would schedule a patient for surgery without preparing the patient to envision the experience that lies before him or her. It is common practice for the medical staff to help the patient anticipate all phases of preparation, surgery, and recovery: describing the protocol during the days and hours preceding surgery, explaining the general steps in the surgical procedure, imagining the recovery room experience, noting the level of pain that can normally be anticipated, projecting the path of postsurgical therapy, and forecasting the stages for long-term recovery. Several sources report that patient stress levels are reduced and recovery hastened when the medical staff prepare the patient to have a realistic understanding of what to expect during the procedures and recovery (Freeman, Dienstbier, Roesch, & Sime, 2000; Leserman, Stuart, Mamish, & Benson, 1989; Markland & Hardy, 1993).

While the medical situation does not perfectly parallel the beginning teacher's situation, the two have this in common: the situations are both very stressful; and without assistance in anticipating the unfamiliar experience, a person's stress is elevated and survival (of one kind or another) is compromised.

Discerning a Pattern of Experiences

We relied on three case studies of first-year teachers, with follow-up interviews of the teachers near the end of their second year of teaching, as a means of mapping a pattern of common experiences for the first-year teacher. Our original protocol called for each of the three researchers to follow a first-year teacher through his or her first year of teaching. We selected the three teachers by taking into account a number of factors. We wanted to have a representative sample of schools and communities. One school we selected was a large high school in a suburb of a large midwestern city. The community consisted of working- and middle-class families. The school, which tracked students into four ability levels in English, had a diverse population with a high percentage of Hispanic American students. A second school, also large, was located in a primarily white, middle-class community in the suburbs of a large midwestern city. The school tracked students into three ability levels.

Our original plan called for the third school to be located in a depressed area with a large minority population. Unfortunately, after a number of failed attempts to schedule interviews at the school with a teacher who had agreed to participate in the study, we had to abandon our attempts to follow this teacher. In the end, we focused on a teacher in another high school in a suburb of a large midwestern city. The community was primarily middle class, with some working-class families. The school had a diverse student population, with a high percentage of Asian American students. The school tracked students into three ability levels.

In selecting teachers for the study, we also wanted a balance of gender and ethnicity. Two of the participants were female and one was male, and one of the women was Asian American. Sharon was the teacher at the large suburban high school with many Hispanic American students. Joshua was our first-year teacher at the suburban high school in a predominantly white, middle-class community; and Lucy was our Asian American teacher at the suburban school with a high percentage of Asian American students.

We recognize that our small sample of teachers and school settings is a limitation of the study. Nevertheless, we believe that the data gathered through these case studies have enabled us to gain considerable insight into the common experiences of first-year English teachers.

Each teacher was to be interviewed five times during the first year of teaching, observed in the classroom twice, and then interviewed a sixth time near the end of the second year of teaching. Lucy, the teacher who was added late in the study, was interviewed in an abbreviated, single but extended interview that took place near the end of her first year of teaching. The attempt was to gather the same information obtained from the other teachers in five sittings. In place of the two classroom observations, with the permission of the subject, we interviewed the teacher's immediate supervisor to confirm the accuracy of the information gathered in the interview and anything important the supervisor had noted in observations from the fall to the spring.

We developed the questions for the interviews based on the results of the survey data on teacher expectations (see Chapter 5) and the concerns that the beginning teachers identified in their initial interviews (see Chapter 3). Each interview had a specific focus (e.g., class management, handling the paper load, supervision/teacher evaluation, etc.). All interviews were audio-recorded and transcribed later. The first interview took place in September; it set the stage for the later interviews and provided some initial information regarding each participant's thoughts and feelings at this early point in the year (see Appendix G for complete questions for each interview). The teachers were questioned about the courses they were teaching and their impressions of the school and students. They were asked to discuss the high point so far, the challenges they faced, and any concerns they had at that point in the year. Interviewers also asked participants to discuss any support they received in and outside the school to help them face the challenges they had identified. Finally, the novice teachers were asked to discuss how well they felt their teacher education program had prepared them for their current teaching experience.

It is important to note that the subjects of the study were given the questions ahead of time to allow them to think about their answers and prepare responses. In all cases, the interviews took place in the schools in which the subjects taught, usually during a planning and/or lunch period or before or after school.

The second interview took place in late October, and it was coupled with the first classroom observation. This interview focused on how the novice teachers were dealing with the curricula they had been assigned to teach. In addition, participants were questioned about how much time they spent preparing lessons and grading papers. Interviewers asked the participants to discuss how the workload was affecting them. The classroom observation focused on classroom management, rapport with students, content knowledge, and use of pedagogy.

The next interview took place in December; at this point, we began to ask the subjects to consider any changes from their responses to our questions in the first two interviews, and to indicate the high point of the teaching experience so far. We also asked them to discuss any challenges they faced and any concerns they had at this point in the year. In addition, we questioned them about any support they were receiving in the school to help them face the challenges. We also asked about any help they might be receiving from outside the school, and we asked them to reflect on how well they thought their university program had prepared them for their current teaching experience.

The fourth interview took place in early March, and like the second interview, this one was coupled with a classroom observation. This interview emphasized supervision and teacher evaluation. We asked the novice teachers to describe their rapport with their supervisors and to describe the teacher evaluation process. We queried them about the extent to which their schools' teacher evaluation programs supported their professional development. In addition, we asked participants to discuss the extent to which their colleagues had been helpful in supporting their development as teachers. We also asked them to discuss the extent to which their teaching experience had changed during the course of the year. We asked them, in answering this question, to consider several topics: their relationships with students, colleagues, supervisors, and parents; handling the workload; command of subject and curriculum; grading and assessment; and their autonomy. In the second observation, we focused on any changes from the first to the second interview.

The fifth interview was conducted in late May. We started this interview by asking participants to reflect on their most memorable experiences during their first year of teaching. We also asked them to reflect on their greatest challenges and to think about what advice they would offer to new teachers who were about to begin their first year of teaching. In addition, we asked the interviewees to consider what advice they would give to school administrators in order to guide their efforts to support new teachers and encourage their retention. Finally, we asked them to think about the advice they would offer directors of teacher training programs to prepare new teachers to enter and remain in the profession.

Once the first-year interviews and observations were completed and the interviews were transcribed, each subject was given a copy of his or her transcribed interviews and asked to read through them and check for accuracy. Each observer then wrote a case study to summarize the experience of the first-year teacher: the observer recorded the setting, noteworthy responses to interview questions, reflections on the classroom observations, and citations from the teacher's reflection on the entire school year.

Once the case studies were written, each interviewee was given a copy of his or her case study and asked to read it over to make sure the case accurately represented what the subject had said in the interviews. With the case studies reviewed and revised by the interviewees, each researcher read all three case studies and wrote a conceptual memo summarizing the common life of the first-year teacher. The three researchers then read all three conceptual memos and sat down to discuss them, looking at similarities and differences. Most striking was the similarity of these conceptual memos. The researchers discussed and reconciled the remaining minor differences. The common life of the first-year teacher discussed in this chapter is a distillation of the essential features that all three researchers identified in their conceptual memos.

Additional Data

In addition to the protocol described for interviewing and observing the first-year teachers, we included one more step. In late April of the academic year following the year we interviewed the first-year teachers, we again contacted the three subjects and asked if we could interview them again in an attempt to get them to reflect on their first two years of teaching. We wanted them to discuss their most memorable experiences and greatest challenges, to identify the most important thing they learned about teaching during their first year of teaching, and to describe how things had changed since our last interview the previous year. Two of the teachers agreed to the follow-up interview: Lucy and Sharon. Joshua failed to return any of our calls or respond to e-mails. Our contacts with administrators at the high school indicated that Joshua was not being rehired for a third year, and we concluded that this was the likely reason he was not interested in being interviewed.

The two remaining teachers were given the interview questions ahead of time, and we interviewed each of them in late April. The interviews were audio-recorded for later transcription. Once the interviews were transcribed, the three researchers read through them and wrote a conceptual memo summarizing the key information. The researchers then sat down together to discuss the memos, looking at the similarities and differences. They discussed similarities and refined minor differences. The common life of the first-year teacher discussed in this chapter also contains the essential features the three researchers identified from these conceptual memos.

The Teachers and Teaching Contexts

Sharon had just turned twenty-three years old during the summer before she started teaching. Her father was in law enforcement, and her parents believed in the value of hard work. As a result, her parents made their children pay for their own college educations. Even though Sharon was in an honors English program at the Midwest suburban high school she attended, she ended up at a nearby community college for her first two years of college before transferring to a large state university to complete her undergraduate degree in English and obtain her teaching certificate.

When Sharon was hired in May, she was given her teaching assignment and the books and other curriculum materials she would need for her classes. She was assigned a mentor, Lori, another teacher in her department. In her first assignment, Sharon taught five classes of tenth graders and had two different preparations. Three of her classes were the tenth-grade "regular" students, and two of her classes were the tenth-grade "below average" students. The English department had four tracks of students and the school had a diverse population, with Hispanic American students composing about 40 percent of the enrollment. Sharon taught all of her classes in one room, which was equipped with current technology: a monitor and videotape player, a computer with Internet connections, and cable TV access. She had two preparation periods.

Although Joshua's parents were not schoolteachers themselves, they did have jobs in education. He thought that the family's involvement in education probably had an influence on his choice of teaching as a career. Joshua attended a competitive private university where he prepared to become an English teacher.

Joshua had been hired in July. At that time, he received his particular teaching assignment and the curriculum materials he would need for his classes. In his first assignment, Joshua taught five classes of ninth graders and had two different preparations, teaching in a suburban high school with a predominantly white enrollment. Three of his classes were the ninth-grade "honors" students, and two of his classes were made up of "regular" ninth graders in a three-track system. In the first semester, he had two preparation periods during the school day; during the second semester, he had only one preparation period because he picked up an assignment as a study hall supervisor. Joshua had no extracurricular responsibilities. He taught all of his classes in one room, which was equipped with current technology: a monitor and videotape player, a computer with Internet connections, and cable TV access. Joshua was assigned a mentor, a colleague from the English department.

Lucy's parents were both immigrants from Southeast Asia. Her father was an engineer and her mother was a nurse. Given this family background, a career in teaching might seem to be the last thing Lucy would decide on. She had attended a reputable high school in the same district where she obtained her teaching position. She had graduated from a competitive public state university with an undergraduate degree in English and speech communications. After graduating, she had worked in the advertising field for a year and a half, and then she decided to obtain her teaching credentials. She then entered a teacher education program at a large religion-affiliated university to obtain her teaching certificate and master's degree in English education.

Lucy was hired at the end of March, and shortly after being hired she received her teaching assignment and the curriculum materials she would need for her classes. She was assigned a mentor, another teacher in the English department. Her teaching assignment consisted of two sections of "regular"-level ninth graders and three sections of "regular"-level eleventh graders in a three-level system. During the spring semester, she lost one section of juniors and picked up a section of an elective speech course, which meant she had three course preparations during the second semester. Lucy was also a coach for cheerleading, an activity that ran from August to April. Teachers did not have their own classrooms, so she taught her classes in three different classrooms. Her rooms were equipped with current technology: a projector with computer hookup, a VCR, and an overhead. If she needed computers for classroom use, she could schedule her classes into one of the school's computer classrooms. The school was a suburban high school near a large midwestern city. Located in a community that was largely middle class, with some working-class families, the school had a diverse student population, with a high percentage of Asian Americans.

School Opens: Exhilaration and Consternation

Our first-year teachers reported that they were thrilled to go to work at the start of the school year, but they also experienced some frustration. As Sharon put it, "I can't believe I'm getting paid for this." She also noted, however, that while her regular students were friendly and most of them did their homework, her below-average students were a bit of a challenge. They did not regularly do their homework, a few students were failing, and they were having difficulties with concepts such as theme; she had to review these concepts frequently and bring in outside materials, such as pop culture, and try new ideas to help them understand. Sharon indicated that the department chair supported her use of new ideas and materials. As a result, she was very "comfortable trying new things," and this made her feel like her chair had confidence in her ability to make wise curricular decisions.

Joshua made similar comments. He noted that his honors students were willing to engage in discussions, and they regularly did their homework. His regular students, however, were reluctant to participate in discussions, and they were less apt to do their homework. He also noted that the regular students needed to be more "concrete" in their discussions and seemed puzzled when discussion moved into abstract areas. One of the high points in the first month of school was that one of his honors classes had become so involved in class discussions that they were managing the discussions themselves and did not have to rely on Joshua as the conduit for assessment and turn taking. He observed, "I didn't have to lead them to things; they are discovering things on their own."

Like her two counterparts, Lucy recalled being "very excited" at the beginning of the school year: "I was so happy to even be at this high school," which she had attended herself and which had a fine reputation, and because "I already knew I was going to help out with cheerleading." Lucy indicated that during the first few weeks of school she felt "so ready," and it was exciting "getting to know the other young, new teachers." But Lucy was frustrated with the ninth-grade curriculum: "The freshman curriculum is set, in that we're all pretty much doing the same thing at the same time." She felt that the curriculum was too restrictive, which made it difficult for her to put her own "creativity into things."

Late September, Early October: End of the Honeymoon

By the end of September and into early October, the first-year teachers were experiencing frustrations that were beginning to take a toll; the honeymoon was clearly over. Joshua, for example, noted that he was frustrated because some students repeatedly reported tardy for class. He felt especially frustrated because he had no sense of a firm schoolwide policy related to tardiness. His other frustration was that the regular students did not actively participate in discussions by responding directly to one another. Instead, these students were more inclined to direct responses to him in a search for validation. These students also discussed concepts in a rather superficial way, when Joshua had hoped he could engage them in exploring concepts in some depth.

Lucy voiced a sentiment shared by all three teachers at this point:

> I kind of laugh because last summer, I convinced myself that I was so ready. . . . I think I did [know what I was doing] for the first three weeks of school, and then all of a sudden I felt like someone pulled something out from underneath me.

She ran out of her daily lesson plans and then realized, "I didn't know what I was doing."

Sharon also expressed frustration. A major difficulty for her was what she described as the "clerical challenges" of the job.

She was particularly frustrated by what she thought was an antiquated attendance system. As she explained, "You have to do it all by hand," and "it takes up a lot of time." Perhaps of greater concern was the fact that the hiring and induction system did not take into account her sense of feeling "unprepared in certain areas"; even though she had questions over the summer, she "had to wait until a week before school started to ask them." She felt particularly frustrated because she had not known that "we didn't have enough books to go around to every student," and she had spent her summer planning units that depended on all students having the books they needed.

Late October, Early November: Debilitating Fatigue

By the time the cold weather had started to settle in to the Midwest, our first-year teachers were experiencing significant difficulties in coping with the challenges they faced. In fact, they were so overwhelmed that the best way to describe what they experienced might be to say that they felt debilitating fatigue. Sharon, for example, maintained that she spent virtually "all [her] time" planning lessons. Furthermore, at this point in the year, she was getting only about five and a half hours of sleep each night because she was staying up late planning lessons for the next day and grading papers.

Sharon indicated that most of October had been particularly difficult for her. She had "lost twenty pounds" since school started. As she explained, "I stand up all day long and I run up and down a third floor of stairs, buzzing around the classroom," and she felt "more tired all the time." On weekends she "could never, never sleep enough." She noted that she started feeling ill in October and observed, "I always have a cold now."

Sharon was also struggling with some of her students around this time: "The honeymoon had worn off for the students." She had had to become more assertive with discipline because some students had started "testing her." One day after she had given a pop quiz, four of her students went to the dean to complain about her. She reported that she was "overwhelmed" that students "didn't work as [she] did when [she] was in high school" and that "education isn't that important to them." She summed up her feelings by saying with dismay, "Oh, my life is a bunch of fifteen-year-olds."

Sharon had to contend with another problem during this period as well, and this problem centered on her appearance. She was an attractive young woman, and a few of the male students in her classes seemed to have a crush on her. She talked the situation over with her department chair. They decided it might be best for her to put her boyfriend's photo on her desk and casually mention that she had a boyfriend. They thought this would put an end to the problem, but in fact the plan backfired: "It kind of turned from being, 'Let's try to be good' to 'She betrayed me. Let's hate her now.'" This seemed to contribute to the general deterioration of her students' classroom behavior. In fact, she said that for a couple of weeks in late October she actually thought to herself, "Well, I should start looking for jobs in January."

Sharon had one additional problem to contend with during this time. She was being observed and evaluated by her department chair and assistant principal for curriculum and instruction. They came to her classroom and observed her "back-to-back." She explained, "This was a little overwhelming, especially because it was the beginning of October, when I was already a little overwhelmed." The observations created problems for her because, as she explained, "I didn't get enough positive feedback from the chair's observation." Sharon lamented that the problem for her and other new teachers is that "[w]e don't know if we're being a good teacher. We need someone to say, 'You're doing a good job.'" This situation caused her so much stress that Sharon approached her department chair to ask him directly, "Am I doing what a first-year teacher should be doing?" Unfortunately, the department chair responded by giving her more "criticism." As a result, she approached the assistant principal to ask him how she was doing. He gave her some very positive feedback, and she said that she "just wanted to breathe, like, a huge sigh of relief." His comment was very important to her because, as a first-year teacher,

> I need to know if I'm being there for these students enough because they're relying on me to teach them English. Am I doing

that? I think I am. But can you tell me if I am? Is this what other people are doing in their classrooms?

The entire observation and evaluation process that took place in October caused Sharon a great deal of stress and anxiety.

Joshua reported that he also was feeling fatigued by early November. His regular students continued to be a challenge. In early November, these students were working with Shakespeare's *The Tempest,* and they were struggling. "It requires me to adjust to the abilities of the students," he noted. "It's hard to tell whether students understand the concepts." He had to spend a great deal of time planning his lessons: "Right now, I need more 'tricks' from a bag of tricks." He observed that the few weeks at the end of October had been especially exhausting: "I wasn't prepared for the physical demands of being on my feet all day and moving around in class." He could count on taking work home every day: "I spend at least two hours per evening in grading and preparing lessons. On weekends, there is usually some work."

Lucy also observed that at this point in the school year she felt quite fatigued. She described her teaching of three sections of eleventh-grade English as "baptism by fire" because she had to mark and grade three sets of research papers at the same time. "It is such a tedious, lockstep unit, and it was just a little overwhelming." In addition, she felt frustrated because "the freshmen curriculum is set, in that we're all pretty much doing the same thing at the same time." There seemed to be little room for creativity. She wondered, "Why do I have to do this? Why can't I just do this my way?"

In addition to dealing with marking and grading large numbers of research papers, Lucy struggled to keep up with planning her lessons. Then she was confronted with midterm examinations and papers to grade, and quarter grades were due. And there was more:

> So November with cheerleading really picking up, football season was over, basketball season was on. They had their competitions. The first set of midterms, and I remember that week clearly, staying very, very late because of the practices and even doing bubble sheets, not realizing that I had to at least have one paper, one test, and several daily grades. I think I was told, but it didn't all register.

She added, "I remember how miserable I was doing the first set of midterms."

Lucy noted that her social life suffered as well, particularly during this difficult period: "Friends were on the side. I have a boyfriend, and he works a lot too, which is a good thing. We both always worked a lot, but even going home, I would be so exhausted that I wouldn't even feel like talking to anyone." She added, "Overall, definitely my social life was put on hold."

January, February: Reenergized

After the winter break, with the bitter cold midwestern winter firmly in place, the three teachers returned to their classrooms reenergized and with a renewed sense of optimism regarding the challenges they would face the rest of the school year. Sharon, for example, felt much more comfortable with the workload: "I am less stressed out, which is good." She added that "winter break was like being reborn. I came back revitalized":

> I feel like a new person. I still hold my same values and beliefs, but I was a different teacher. I had more confidence. I knew I had better command of the curriculum, and I didn't spend all of winter break doing schoolwork. I was doing other things, and it was doing those other things that made me more adult or made me more teacher[-ish] or something.

She reported feeling "more like the other teachers."

Sharon also considered the winter break a major turning point in terms of the curriculum:

> I spent some of winter break figuring out where we were as a class, what we were doing, and where we were going, and how we were going to get there. That helped take me out of the day-by-day lesson planning stress and [allowed me to] look at the big picture.

Lucy reported that she felt revitalized after the winter break, as well as more comfortable with her students: "I loosened up a little bit" and "wasn't so uptight about every little thing." After the break, "It wasn't like [the fall] so much," in part because she relaxed and became "more flexible." A challenge for her was dealing with the average kids. She had trouble being "consistent" with them about discipline, but she talked with her mentor teacher about how to handle particular situations and got some helpful advice about what she should do about "disciplining" students. The break was also a welcome relief because she had not been prepared for the time required to get everything done: "I do enjoy what I do, but it is just the time commitment, the lack of sleep, and just often being in the building too much." She added,

> What I found myself doing a lot was just staying after school and just working until five or six, eating and then going to [cheerleading] practice because I felt that there was always work to do. I felt it would be wasting time going home and coming back, so often I did stay straight here several nights in a row.

Lucy indicated that she also spent too much time on grading: "I think maybe at the beginning of the year, I had probably spent more time than necessary with comments and things." In the fall, she had attended a conference sponsored by the area English teachers association, and as she commented, "The conference made me think about different ways that I could grade." As a result of what she learned at the conference, she began to spend much less time evaluating student writing. The winter break provided Lucy with the time to put these new ideas into practice.

Joshua also reported feeling revitalized after the winter break. He was pleased by the apparent growth in his ninth graders. "At the start, they didn't know what they were doing. They didn't know how to work with a text or prepare for a test. The students are progressing in making the transition from middle school to high school." He reported, however, feeling frustrated because he did not have the benefit of experience from which to draw on when making decisions about lessons and about what actions to take. As he put it, "I don't have the benefit of experience to know what kind of prep work will get students toward the end goal."

Joshua was concerned about the lack of collaboration in his department: "Collaboration would be nice. We wrote a common final. I would like to collaborate and agree on where we are going with the curriculum. Basically, I would like some validation for what I am doing."

Like his counterparts, Joshua needed the rest over break because the fatigue of the job continued to be a challenge: "Being on my feet all day is physically fatiguing, which I didn't expect." He realized he needed to prepare himself better in order to correct some of his problems. "Sleeping more would be helpful. Grading and planning takes up most of your time outside of the classroom. Physically, you have to *train* for it."

The three teachers reflected on how their university programs had prepared them for the job of teaching English in high school. Lucy, for example, noted, "I thought my university had a pretty solid program. I was pretty happy with it. They were kind of hands-on, and I did have to design my own portfolios and lesson plans, and I did a lot of activities." She added, "I felt that the activities were good, overall very positive." Sharon felt that her teacher education program had prepared her "very well," but she firmly believed there were some glaring shortcomings: "In general, I think that all colleges should require a special ed class. I would also include some sort of ESL training optional to those who know they will teach in a diverse area." Such a course should cover all types of inclusion, she said, because of the range of students she had encountered in her classes.

Joshua held a very different opinion of his teacher education program:

> The university program is not very good. Grades and parent phone calls—they did help about that. We did some role playing, had field experience and parents as guest speakers. As far as the fifty minutes when I have each group of kids, they were not helpful. Having a particular bag of tricks, they were not helpful. They advised us appropriately about the attitude we should take with kids. In our methods course, we didn't need as much scaffolding to help us through the materials.

In brief, the mode of instruction in their methods courses did not model how to work with students who might have some trouble learning. The methods students themselves were college seniors who needed little assistance with learning. As methods students, then, our participants did not see realistic scenes of teachers accommodating challenged learners.

March: Hope Springs Eternal

All three of the first-year teachers reported that by March, with the hint of spring in the air, they felt comfortable with their respective department chairs. Their chairs encouraged them to try out their ideas in the classroom as long as they remained true to the guiding principles of the curriculum. Joshua expressed this idea best by saying that he felt free and comfortable in "bouncing ideas" off of the department chair. His relationship with the chair had evolved into a "teacher-to-teacher" relationship. In fact, he indicated that the department chair had influenced his thinking in various ways: "He influenced me to take more of a constructivist approach" to teaching. The department chair encouraged him to "search for an expanded repertoire" and use "lots of group work" in his teaching. Similarly, Lucy described her department chair as "friendly, helpful, and supportive." By March she felt comfortable talking about teaching ideas with her chair, whom she respected, and she observed that the chair's assessment of her teaching "matters" a great deal to her.

The first-year teachers reported that the teacher evaluation process was a positive aspect of their teaching experience. The evaluation process at Lucy's school, for example, required five classroom observations of the first-year teacher: two by the principal and three by the department chair. Most of these required a preobservation conference, a classroom observation, and a postobservation conference. She felt that the principal and assistant principal were more interested in ensuring that she was a "professional" and that she had control of "classroom management." In contrast, the department chair was most interested in the same things that were "important to her." As she explained, "I care a thousand times more what she thinks" because "we share the freshman curriculum," because she is my "direct supervisor," and because of her "background" in the subject area. Sharon made an important observation about the evaluation process that all three teachers seemed to share: "No one likes to be put under a microscope and/or be scrutinized. However, it is important to learn that any good administrator is just trying to help teachers improve." Sharon felt that the evaluation process at her school "was a very supportive system." She commented, "I thought that they are doing a great job of supporting me and answering my questions."

The first-year teachers reported valuing the help they received from their mentors and felt that the mentoring system was helpful and supported their efforts. Joshua, for example, said that the school had assigned him to an experienced teacher within the same department. He had "regular conversations" with his mentor, and these conversations provided him with "help" in a variety of areas. He noted, however, that the biggest problem was having time for collaboration. Getting access to his mentor and other colleagues was a challenge, and he often had to rely on e-mail to stay in contact with other teachers.

Sharon offered the clearest explanation of how important the mentoring system was to these three teachers. Like the other two teachers, she was assigned a mentor in her own department. Her mentor teacher, Lori, was "always there when I need[ed] her." Two weeks after Sharon became convinced that she would not survive October, she finally told her mentor how she was feeling. Lori helped her through that most difficult period, helping her to manage her time better, especially when it came to grading papers. She recalled: "My mentor really helped a lot because she said, 'When you're grading papers, you know, don't spend fifteen minutes, twenty minutes on each paper.'" Lori showed her the importance of "just keying in on certain things and checking for that" instead of trying to mark every error in every student paper. According to Sharon, receiving this kind of practical and helpful advice led her to conclude that the mentoring system at her school was "awesome."

Receiving help from mentors is only part of the story for these three teachers. As previously noted, each received considerable support from a department chair, as well as from other administrators. In addition, they got considerable help from colleagues. Lucy noted, "Everyone [in the department] was very generous with sharing materials." She indicated that the friendly staff, effective mentoring program, and helpful colleagues in English were valuable supports that helped her make the adjustments to her new workplace. Sharon made similar comments about her colleagues and others in her school. She also developed a positive relationship with an older teacher in her department who gave her considerable help and guidance. As she explained, Gary

> has, like, taken me under his wing and, you know, he always asks me questions about my weekend, and I like to know what his family is doing. He is kind of like a father figure at work for me. . . . I like having somebody watching out for me, making sure I am not being walked all over, so I really respect him.

In addition to receiving help from colleagues, the three first-year teachers reported receiving varying degrees of support from other sources. Joshua, for example, indicates that he got considerable support from his father. Although his father was not a classroom teacher, he had some experience working in education. Joshua found that he could go to his father to solicit advice, seek validation, and vent about his problems and concerns.

Sharon identified a number of people as sources of help from outside the school. Her boyfriend, a first-year English teacher at another high school, was the primary person she could talk with about her problems and concerns. She also relied at times on her family, primarily her mother and father; "other teacher friends" from her teacher education program; and "former professors from [her] teacher education program." Finally, Sharon identified an unexpected source of help: the interviewing process with the researcher. In talking about the interviews, she reported, "I learned a lot, and thanks again. This really helps me, when I sit down to answer these questions. It turns into more of a diary or a journal." Sharon described the interview sessions as "therapeutic." She elaborated:

> You have to listen to me, kind of, for an important reason. Whereas if I talk to my mentor, I could spend forever talking about it and it is good reflection for me, but it is nice to have somebody like you to be there listening and validating what I

say, not because you are getting paid for it but because it is something you are interested in and you are studying and it makes my feelings validated.

Lucy also received support from a number of people, but she had a difficult problem to deal with in terms of family support. Lucy had contact through e-mail with a first-year teacher who had been in her teacher education program. She also kept in touch with a friend who taught at another high school in the same school district. She communicated and discussed "shared experiences" with these people. In addition, she received support from friends and former co-workers from the business world. Although Lucy lived at home with her parents and had a boyfriend, she did not initially receive the kind of support she needed from them: "They initially had a lack of understanding of the time that was involved with teaching. They didn't see teaching beyond a 7:30 a.m. to 3:30 p.m. job." Her boyfriend would even say to her when she was working on a lesson, "Come on! Just put that down, it'll be fine. It is just one day." As a result, "It was kind of touchy in the beginning."

Even in March, our three teachers continued to find the workload daunting. Joshua called the workload "overwhelming" still but noted that he brought on himself much of the work because he was inclined to "collect and grade everything." Lucy indicated that the workload was still difficult: "the biggest thing" she really hadn't expected was "the time spent" trying to do everything. "I knew it would be intense," she added, "but not as intense at certain times of the year because of cheerleading, because of the weird hours, and everything else." Lucy also admitted that she brought some of the work on herself: "I spend too much time writing comments on their papers," and "I did volunteer" for the extracurricular activities. Sharon expressed similar feelings about the workload, saying that if she could change one thing about her job it would be grading papers: "I absolutely hate grading papers." She went on to say, "I love teaching, but the paperwork drives me nuts. Sometimes it is so brainless that it kills me, and other times (like grading essays) it is so time-consuming that I want to scream."

April: False Hope, the Cruelest Month

By late April or early May, when spring was in full bloom, our three first-year teachers reflected on the experience of the entire school year. Sharon articulated the feelings of all three. She noted that she had returned from spring break "energized" because she had realized that the "long haul [was] over," but the return from spring break also turned out to be one of her major challenges. She began a countdown of the last nine weeks and then realized that was a "bad idea" because by week five she "was ready to be done." She added, "I just feel washed out in an okay way, drained from the experience, just back-to-back new things." For Lucy, the challenge was the time required for cheerleading. "I don't think I truly realized how much time I'd give to cheerleading." The time she spent on extracurricular activities was a major drain on her energy, and ultimately this energy drain had a negative impact on her social life. She literally had no time for family, friends, or her boyfriend: "I felt my boyfriend resented me because all I cared about was school and that I didn't give him enough of my time."

Joshua discussed two challenges that frustrated him. One major challenge was maintaining orderly discussions. In some of his classes, the students did not embrace the idea of taking turns contributing to discussions. He also had to contend with the growing mounds of papers: "I don't want to assign less. I don't know how to reduce the paper load and still make the assignments that students need." He noted that as the year progressed, the paper load had increased "exponentially."

Despite the difficulties and challenges these teachers faced during the year, they all reported ending the year on a positive note. Lucy, for example, indicated that she was very happy with her work and her accomplishments, especially during the second semester: "That is when I got good at turning in the midterm reports, and I got good at turning around things much better with papers and organizing. I really started to see the end of the year." She added, "I was really happy in terms of the curriculum. I had a lot of fun. I really liked all the literary works." Sharon noted that despite feeling "tired" and drained of energy, she was beginning to feel a little "sentimental" about the school year coming to an end: "I will miss these guys" because "they're my first batch of students." Joshua assumed a significant extracurricular responsibility for the second semester, devoting four to five hours a day to this extra responsibility. He expressed the hope that matters would be better in the future: "[I] saved all lessons electronically so that I can 'tweak' the assignments instead of writing whole lessons."

Reflections on the First Year

In reflecting on their experiences, the three teachers made some suggestions for other first-year teachers. Joshua had three suggestions: (1) Engage in no extracurricular responsibility until spring. During the first month of school, he "came home each night and collapsed with exhaustion." (2) "Attend to little management challenges immediately before the problem grows." He added, "It is more difficult to reclaim a class by becoming suddenly draconian." (3) "Prepare for the physical grind."

Sharon added two interesting recommendations for beginning teachers: (1) "Don't try to be popular." Even though she did not need to learn this the hard way, she still had to deal with students who "assumed that I would be the 'cool teacher.'" She reported having to tell them that "I do not wish to be a part of all that drama twice in my life" before her students finally backed off. (2) It is important for new teachers to "smile" and "be happy to be at school even when you are tired, even when your lesson bombs first hour, even when you feel sick." (3) New teachers need to remember that they "are the adults" and were "once teens, too." New teachers, she added, should do their best to "appreciate" teenagers for who they are.

Lucy had her students evaluate her teaching. Based on the results of their evaluations, she offered the following advice to beginning teachers: (1) Don't talk down to students. Lucy's students "appreciated that because I'm a younger teacher . . . I didn't talk to them like they were babies." (2) Make instruction more student centered than teacher centered. Her students liked the fact that she "didn't just lecture" and that she "always got down to business, yet they were allowed to have fun and always knew they could come to [her] for help." (3) New teachers should not try to please everyone. She explained, "In the beginning I was very concerned about what everyone else would think in terms of rules, that I was doing everything right, even down to the attendance sheets, my books, wanting everything to be perfect on paper, my procedures, and even my students." As a result, she was "more rigid" in her classes than she needed to be.

Based on their experiences, two of the first-year teachers had some suggestions for what school administrators could do to help beginning teachers. Joshua pointed to two areas in which school administration could help beginning teachers. First, he would like for new teachers to have some help in managing classes. He reported that the school's discipline policies and procedures offered teachers few options for contending with students who posed discipline challenges. Joshua also wished that school administration would structure time for teachers to collaborate with other department members. He was especially interested in having time to meet regularly with other teachers who taught the same subjects, so that he could share ideas and assignments.

Sharon also had some advice for what school administrators could do to help beginning teachers. She noted that "August and September are not the only times that new teachers need information and support." She felt "overloaded with pamphlets, papers, binders, charts, and color-coded folders, etc." from various committees and departments, and she felt "lost in a mess of information." As she explained, "It was all too much at the wrong time, and I just packed it into the top of my closet at home"; the administration should "give it to the teacher when hired." That way, she noted, "I could have studied it all summer if I wanted." She added, "I don't have time to search through the table of contents in five different color-coded binders."

Sharon also believed that school administration could do much more to help new teachers with the ESL and special education programs. These programs, she said, really "need to take the initiative" and actually "go into the new teacher's classroom and meet eye-to-eye in September, October, and again in November, maybe even January too." She added, "I knew I needed to know these people, but I was unsure who to contact and didn't want to insult anyone" because "I didn't know or was unsure of their names." She believed that her ESL and special education students "would have done better academically if [she] had felt comfortable knowing who to approach with questions."

Based on their experiences, two of the first-year teachers had some suggestions for what teacher education programs could do to help beginning teachers. Joshua expressed some criticism of his university training to become a teacher:

> They assumed that we knew pedagogy, so they emphasized peripheral issues, like how to respond to an angry parent and theoretical issues about curriculum. What was lacking was a proactive effort to show how teachers function in the classroom. For example, no one discussed how to write a test. In the observations that we did, you watched a lot but didn't spend much time talking about how the teacher was thinking. As another example, the university instructors did not train students in how to facilitate discussions.

Sharon had one suggestion for how teacher training programs might provide additional support for beginning teachers: teacher education programs should "go the extra mile to offer continued support even after the student has graduated." She believed that teacher education programs could do more to keep in contact with students once they graduate and provide support as they begin their teaching careers.

April: One Year Later

When our beginning teachers had nearly another year of teaching experience behind them, two of them spoke with us to reflect on their experiences and how things had or had not changed since we interviewed them a year earlier. Both of these teachers could point to memorable experiences. What struck Lucy the most was that simply moving from the first year to the second year was memorable: "I came in and I was, like, people kind of know me here. They're saying hi to me or they remember me, and I just remember the [first] year being a blur." She was surprised by "just that, and seeing students that I wasn't even aware that they had maybe felt like they did enjoy my class" and "[I did have] maybe somewhat of an impact" on them. She explained, "that is what I so badly wanted. Why did I come into teaching? Being able to have, even on a few students, that kind of impact." She also noted being struck by how difficult it was to balance teaching and coaching cheerleading. "I remember, just with cheerleading, just the craziness of some days and the scheduling, and I remember, you know, the state weekends, just how crazy that was, too."

Sharon could also point to memorable experiences. Most memorable for her was coming to terms with the fact that "my students had such screwed-up home lives, and not just my students but kids today in general." Another memorable experience for Sharon was calling a student's home for the first time. She was concerned about how her students would react when she called: "when I did call home for the first time, the student actually came in the next day and thanked me for calling home, which was so sweet, and that really gave me confidence about calling home, and he said that that gave him a wake-up call." Sharon began attending graduate school for an administrative degree. "I started graduate school and I loved it. Why that's memorable to me is because I love school and I miss being a student." She called the program "neat" and was "excited about it."

Sharon reported being quite excited because she had won the NCTE Leadership Development Award, underwritten by Pearson Prentice Hall Education, which supported her in attending the National Council of Teachers of English (NCTE) Annual Convention. In addition, she gave a presentation at the annual state conference of teachers of English and at the NCTE Annual Convention. She explained, "I felt like I was among the younger ones and the most inexperienced at the conference. But I felt like I wanted to be and needed to be [there], and I felt welcomed by the people there." She described the professional experience as "awesome," and she even submitted a proposal for another presentation for the next year.

Both of these beginners reported facing new challenges during their second year of teaching. Lucy was shocked at the number of special education students she had in many of her classes: "Last year, for whatever reason, I swear that I felt like I only had maybe just one kid in every class that had an IEP." In her second year, however, "every class it seems like I have a handful of kids" with IEPs. "I didn't have to deal with this last year." In addition to the significant increase in the number of special education students she had to contend with, Lucy was assigned to teach sophomore honors, and this proved to be a real challenge: "I just remember open house being intimidating because the room was packed—mom and dad of the accelerated kids, and I wasn't used to that." These parents were much different from the parents of her first-year regular students the previous year: "I've had some crazy ones, really demanding parents. You know, 'What grade does my son have today?'" One parent became so demanding that "she got the counselor involved," and Lucy asked her department chair and other teachers who taught the course for assistance with the mother. She reached a point during the first quarter when she briefly thought, "I'm not cut out to teach this, and I don't want to teach it."

In some ways, Sharon's second-year challenges mirrored those of Lucy. Like Lucy, Sharon was assigned to teach two classes of enriched sophomore students. She was excited about it, but, like Lucy, on parent open house night she found herself embroiled in a conflict with some of the parents of these students: "I got practically pushed into a corner by angry parents." The parents were upset because

> their students didn't do well [in class] and they paid for it, and their parents were very angry, and I explained the situation to them. They didn't literally push me, but I had to explain that I am not changing my mind. [The students] can do the work the way it is supposed to be done, or they can receive the consequences for it.

Like Lucy, Sharon ultimately needed some help: "I had to have my department chair step in with one, just one. I've had a great year other than that."

Gaining Confidence

One of the things that stood out for the researchers is that these two teachers were gaining in confidence after their first year of experience, and the teachers recognized this as well. As Sharon noted when talking about starting graduate school and presenting at conferences:

> I've gained more confidence and I really like the people I work with. I've gotten to know them better now that we're all shoved into the English office, and I am able to get to know them better as people, not just teachers. I think that's been able to help me grow as a professional, too, because anytime any of us has an idea or a question, we just bounce it off of each other.

Lucy identified her own growing confidence in terms of the challenges she faced with the parents of accelerated students:

> You can't be Teacher of the Year the first couple of years; you can't do it all. I am more of an idealist and I have this picture of everything that you want to do, and you just have to celebrate things that you have accomplished; and in already looking back, I know I am getting better. I know I am. Even in small ways, even though there are challenges, like all the accelerated kids and all the IEPs. Now, I can say too that I don't know if you could do it in the first year, but in the second year really try to give yourself opportunities to have fun. You can have a little fun your first year, when you can catch your breath. But really, already second year you have more of an inner peace. I noticed that in myself.

Learning How to Teach

Both teachers had learned some important things about how to teach. Sharon noted that now when she plans a lesson, "I think of why I'm doing something or how to go about a lesson to always keep the students in mind first." She added,

> Whenever I'm deciding whether or not I should teach a book or whether or not I should make this certain choice with a lesson, it's always, "How are [the students] going to benefit?" Not, "Do

I want to teach this because it's fun to teach?" But it's like, "Is it meaningful? Does it matter to them somehow?" I already knew that that was a good thing to do, but it's harder to do than it is to say you're supposed to do this.

Lucy made similar comments about what she had learned about teaching. Teaching accelerated students has helped her to "anticipate" what students might ask: "So when I'm preparing lessons, it's like I always have to think of particular people in class," and she asks herself, "What is this person going to ask?" She also felt that she is doing better at "planning for a unit." She noted, "I am able to look at units in a way that's more thematic":

> I'm actually looking at my units, my junior units, and saying, "It's kind of making sense." I'm really feeling like I'm curriculum planning. Like I'm not just doing this because I was asked to do this, but it's coming together and it's making sense and it's coming together like a puzzle. I'm shaping it and I feel like I'm having more control. I'm definitely feeling not like I'm just surviving but I'm feeling like I'm contributing by doing these lesson plans.

How New Teachers Would Advise Themselves

Both of the teachers had some advice for those just beginning their teaching careers, and both were reflective enough to know what they would do differently if they could begin their teaching experience again. Sharon remembered her "really awful" November during her first year, advising, "Don't give up if you feel overwhelmed." In reflecting on this difficult time, she noted, "I was just so stressed out, [but] now I definitely don't want to quit. I can understand why I felt that way, but it's just a shock to me that I was ever at that low of a point at such an early part of my career":

> I think the profession loses a lot of good teachers because they do not get the support that they need in the first few years. I think that the support that I received kept me going—not that I would quit, because I'm not a quitter, but I might have been in that low point for a lot longer. And maybe that might have changed my mind about other decisions.

In discussing the advice she would offer new teachers, Lucy quickly responded, "You can't please everyone." She went on to say,

> This year really helped me better fine-tune my own morals and ethics in the classroom. And I don't think last year I really thought about it as much, unless I was forced to, but now having gone through that first year and looking back, I really had to answer those questions and situations. So that idea that you can't please everyone, and you still have to keep organized and balanced, and you're still going to have nights where you are up very late.

Both teachers' comments support the advice of new teachers in general: expect growth and improvement, don't give up hope, take care of your health, seek out the advice and assistance of others, expect to spend long hours planning and grading papers, and don't expect to have much of a social life.

The comments of these two teachers offer food for thought for teacher educators. It is important to be aware of the way in which new teachers view their own needs and their own means of coping. Understanding these perspectives may help teacher educators better prepare new teachers for the realities of the classroom and provide meaningful support for them once they enter the classroom.

Advice for School Administrators

These two teachers had some advice for school administrators to help guide their efforts to support new teachers and encourage their retention. According to Sharon, schools should "invest in a solid mentoring program. . . . My advice is don't just throw together a haphazard program just to be able to say, 'We have a mentoring program.' Really take the time to do it right; otherwise, don't do it at all." She explained,

> I have a few friends in other schools where they're also involved in mentoring programs which aren't as consistent and as helpful as the one I had here [at this school]. And I think that it is very important that administrators take the time to give that support

to teachers and provide solid mentors who really want to do it, not because there's a stipend involved or because they have to, but because they're truly interested in making their department a better place.

Lucy also felt that her interaction with colleagues and administrators was a key to her growth. The support she received from her department chair and other colleagues was "terrific." In fact, one of her colleagues who taught honors students for many years was very supportive of her when she was having difficulties. This teacher reminded Lucy that when the teacher first started teaching she had "parents run over [her] and kids think that they could." Lucy commented, however, that school leaders should "practice what they preach." She felt that she was not supported when she had followed all of the correct procedures on a student who was continually truant: "I thought it was taken care of, and then the student returned to my class when the student should have been dropped." The end result was that the student actually "yelled at [her]," and when she talked to the administrator, he seemed to dismiss her concerns.

Advice for Teacher Education Programs

Both of our teachers had some specific advice for teacher training programs to help them prepare new teachers to enter and remain in the profession. Lucy had specific recommendations regarding observations in pre–student teaching and student teaching experiences: "I know a lot of students—and I know that I did this too—just were getting hours to get hours. So maybe have more of a definitive goal, like this is what you need to accomplish." In other words, "maybe [observations] could have been more valuable if perhaps [they were] more guided." Sharon offered the following suggestion for teacher training programs: "You really need to do a lot of work after students graduate." She added, "I remember asking, 'What do I want? I want universities to be more supportive of their graduates.' I have definitely received that support."

Projection and Promise for New Teachers

The cases of these three teachers provide a small sample from which to generalize about the common experience of all beginning high school English teachers. We obviously have not accounted for teachers in all settings, with all student populations, and in all school cultures. We are struck, however, by the similarities between the stories of our subjects and by the similarities in the pattern of experience that each of the three researchers noted among the case studies. We again urge beginning teachers, their university instructors, their mentors, and their supervisors to become familiar with this common pattern of experience to help beginners project the possibilities for the first school year. If the medical analogy with which we began this chapter holds up, it makes good sense to make the unfamiliar and unknown territory of teaching a little less foreign through a projection of the experiences that new teachers commonly have. We return to the idea that frustrations stem in large measure from the shock of unexpected experiences; a review of the typical pattern of the school year can ease the jolt and instill some confidence in beginning teachers.

The Benefits of Experience

The survey results we report in Chapter 5 reveal several distinctions between experienced teachers and those university students who are training to become teachers. The survey responses indicate that, with one notable exception, experienced teachers are far more confident than preservice teachers about a number of issues related to their teaching. After studying the survey results, we conducted interviews with six experienced teachers to attempt to trace what happens to veteran teachers over time to make them distinct from new teachers. We also asked why new teachers aren't more like the experienced teachers they admire. The simple answer is this: experienced teachers have the benefit of *experience*. Of course, the response is circular or redundant. The simple response prompts other questions: What does *experience* mean? What benefits can experience provide? What kinds of experiences helped to shape the veteran teachers, and how did the experiences influence them?

The analysis in this chapter derives from three sources of data: (1) transcripts of six interviews (one each with six experienced teachers), (2) experienced teachers' written analyses of seven problem-based scenarios, and (3) first-year teachers' analyses of the differences between their responses to problem-based situations and the experienced teachers' responses to the same situations. (See Appendix H for the protocol for interviewing experienced teachers and Appendixes E and F for the scenarios.) Three outside readers read the transcripts and identified a pattern of change that the experienced teachers report has occurred over time. In completing their analysis, the readers responded to two central questions (see Appendix I for the complete set of instructions): (1) In <u>what ways</u> have teachers changed from their first year of teaching to the current year, after they have taught for at least ten years? (2) According to the experienced teachers, what has <u>influenced</u> or <u>caused</u> their change over the years?

In their responses to the problem-based scenarios, the experienced teachers described how they would have responded to the situation as a beginning teacher and how they would respond now. These teachers also explained any change in their approach, from their first year to the current year. We draw from their comments as a means of explaining their change over the years.

The earlier survey results (see Chapter 5) point to six specific areas of difference between the beginning teacher and the experienced teacher. The following analysis focuses on those six categories. Table 7.1 provides a summary of differences between new and experienced teachers in six areas of new teachers' concerns.

Classroom Management/Relationships with Students

Experienced teachers recall that as beginning teachers they felt compelled to come on strong to impress upon students that the teacher was indisputably in charge. Some teachers could capitalize on being physically intimidating. Some teachers relied on a rigid set of rules and consequences. Some teachers simply yelled a lot. As new teachers, they remembered their own teachers as being rather strict authoritarians. One teacher recalls, "I guess I must have felt that that was the way it was supposed to be." The same teacher characterizes the change this way: "I gradually worked out of that because I felt more confident in myself as a teacher. And it's probably more now of an attitude like, 'Okay, what are we going to do? How are we going to achieve what we need to do?'"

The sense of confidence in who they are as teachers moves the experienced teachers away from authoritarian rule toward a more negotiated understanding of the expectations for the class. One teacher recognized that he had a physically imposing presence from the beginning of his career. He initially depended on this physical advantage, but he changed his classroom persona over time. Another teacher describes the change in this way:

TABLE 7.1. Summary of Contrasts between New and Experienced Teachers

Areas of Concern	The New Teacher	The Veteran Teacher
Classroom Management	Emphasizes a need to control behavior through the imposition of rules and punishments.	Emphasizes the need to form positive relationships with students through the expression of the importance of the class, the support of the teacher, and the teacher's expectation that the students will succeed.
Handling the Workload	Demands many written assignments and tries to evaluate each one in great detail.	Follows a deliberate process for the completion of each project, with an emphasis on the process rather than the accumulation of finished products.
Grading/ Evaluation	Relies on frequent assessments and has great faith that the numbers in the grade book represent an accurate and reliable measure.	Relies on a limited number of key assessments, and exercises flexibility and the consideration of multiple factors in making judgments.
Relationship with Supervisor	Worries about the judgments the supervisor might make and is hesitant to tell the supervisor about difficulties.	Feels confident about the working relationship with the supervisor and is aware and confident of his or her own strengths.
Autonomy	Feels fairly confident that he or she has control of the curriculum but is unsure of what to do. Does not make contributions that affect the department or program as a whole.	Feels confident about autonomy and knows the connections with the larger program. Can identify his or her specific contributions to the department or program.
Physical Appearance; Personal Characteristics	Is very conscious of his or her physical characteristics and how they might support or inhibit the ability to do the job.	Relies on establishing an environment in which there is a shared sense of the mission for the class and respect for the individual goals of each class member.

It is very good to talk about what your goals and expectations are with the students. And come to a set of expectations together. Tell them, "Certainly I can add something to this list," make them so it is more of a committee experience rather than a teacher telling them what to do.

The experienced teachers have their rules, but the dictation of rules is not the first order of business in their classes. Some teachers report that they involve the students in compiling standards for behavior in the classroom because the students are sensitive to operating in an orderly environment. As one teacher reports:

When I first managed a class, I came in with all of these rules about what they should and shouldn't do. And I think it was because I was worried that the department would get a sense that I didn't know how to manage the class. Now I think it is because of my age and raising two kids through high school and college. I think it has changed so that I am much more laid back with them. They create their own goals and expectations, and we talk about that at the beginning of the year. And we come to some sort of agreement.

The experienced teachers report becoming less rigid over time. In part, they are less rigid because they became more confident in who they are as teachers and less concerned about how others will judge them. They have an understanding of a professional standard and can monitor for themselves how they measure up to the standard. The experienced teachers also report that they change as they develop more empathy for the students. For some teachers, empathy develops quickly when they see how their own children are affected by some questionable practices in schools.

The advice that experienced teachers offer, then, runs counter to the conventional wisdom. *Whereas beginning teachers might feel inclined to begin the school year by impressing upon students a set of rules and the consequences of violating those rules, the veteran teachers describe an approach that emphasizes identifying the goals of the course, outlining teacher expectations, expressing confidence in the students' ability to attain the goals, and demonstrating willingness to help any students who have difficulty.*

Grading Papers and Handling the Workload

The experienced teachers recall that as new teachers they thought they were supposed to grade every assignment and every piece of paper to which a student attached a name. Over time they realized they could rely on fewer products as indicators of students' development. Some of the experienced teachers recall that when they were new teachers, the veteran teachers shared with them the fact that they did not need to grade every piece of paper students wrote on. They found ways to give students credit for having completed assignments, but they reserved any kind of analytical grading for those times when students turned in extended writing that may have developed through multiple drafts.

One of the time-consuming elements of grading papers is feeling a need to be able to defend assigned grades. One teacher reports: "There was a sense early on, too, I think, at times I needed to be able to defend a grade, and that's not really a concern now." This defense involved an ongoing internal dialogue with some imagined critic—perhaps a student or a parent. Not only were the teachers thinking about how to judge the quality of the work, but they were also imagining explaining to someone else how they had made their judgments.

Judgments about the quality of student work evolved over time as well. One teacher describes the challenge: "I had a while to get comfortable with what was a quality essay and how I determined what a quality essay was." Over time the teachers see many student papers and have a firm idea about the range of performance. A teacher can become a much more efficient grader and much more confident about making judgments. Another experienced teacher reflects:

> You could, once you start reading, you kind of, you kind of have a pretty good feeling for the quality level of an essay after the first page because you've been down that road so many times and the syntax, and vocabulary, and the argument, and the rhetoric, and the style, and those components are fairly evident after a page.

While the experienced teachers report that they become more efficient at grading papers over time, they find the assessment of students has become more difficult:

> I have more difficulty now trying to figure out a grade. I can tell
> an A paper from an F paper, but a B, C? Middle ground is kind of
> hard to handle sometimes. I kind of stress over that, in that I
> think, "OK, this could make a difference in the kid's GPA. His
> whole life is at stake for this one *Macbeth* paper."

In a technical sense, teachers find grading easier, and they devise
some time management strategies for handling the grading load.
At the same time, the teachers report becoming more sensitive to
the impact that decisions about grades have on their students. In
part, the sensitivity derives from developing an understanding
and appreciation of the adolescents with whom they work. The
process may be accelerated by having children of their own and
seeing firsthand how grades affect the lives of their children. Here
is one teacher's reflection:

> Well, part of it is just being around kids for so long. And the
> other thing is raising your own kids. I saw some things with my
> own children that I thought were appalling, especially when my
> daughter was in junior high. They used to—they had a ridicu-
> lous grading scale. She would always fall short, mathematically,
> one one-hundredth of a point, you know, and they would never
> give her the higher grade.

The idea that someone could split hairs about a grade and be-
grudge a student a higher grade seemed inherently unfair and
hurtful to this teacher. In turn, she did not want to be guilty of
the same practices with the students in her own classes. *In general, then, the experienced teachers report that over time they
have gained a greater understanding of adolescents and have become more empathetic.*

Relationship with Supervisor

The experienced teachers recall that at the beginning of their careers they were concerned about keeping their jobs by complying
with the expectations of their supervisors. One teacher describes
this attitude: "I just wanted to do what was expected of me, try

to fulfill the requirements of the job, and stay alive from semester to semester, year to year, and those type of things." Over time, teachers become more knowledgeable about the standards for performance, more confident in their abilities, and more comfortable about being judged competent professionals. According to another teacher, the change involves "more sharing of ideas about teaching, and about literature, and about writing."

The interviewees remember that as beginning teachers they were open to having a supervisor tell them what he or she wanted them to do so that they could comply. Initially, they were guarded about revealing much about what they were doing in classes and what their experience of being a teacher was like. Here is one teacher's memory of the early period of her career:

> I really got very used to the evaluation process, but I don't feel that I was ever really able to share my concerns with my supervisors because I saw instances where those concerns showed up on other people's evaluations. So truthfully whenever anybody asked to help me, when supervisors in the beginning asked me how things were going, I said, "Wonderful." They said, "Oh, did you cover that?" And I would be like, "Oh, yeah." You know, it was a game.

Although the teachers were initially cautious and distant with supervisors, as they grew in experience they developed a collegial relationship. The experienced teachers knew they had knowledge about their subject, about pedagogy, about the students, and about the school. The supervisor became the colleague with whom the teachers exchanged ideas. In some cases, as supervisors came and went, the teachers were in the position of being more knowledgeable about the school and the community and could advise the supervisor. One teacher reported this change in the relationship with supervisors:

> I think it has changed a lot. I think that I really pretty much can say whatever, tactfully, what I think, and I have because I think people appreciate the honesty. And I think that part of it is as you grow older, you learn that you get certain respect for your age.

Curriculum Planning and Classroom Autonomy

From the very beginning of their careers, the experienced teachers recognized that they had a good deal of autonomy in their own classrooms, although the extent of each teacher's autonomy was bound by the culture of individual schools. At the same time that teachers had substantial autonomy, they also wanted to satisfy the expectations of a supervisor. They could, however, report that they were following an existing curriculum and covering whatever material the supervisor expected them to cover. One experienced teacher reports on his work with the curriculum in his first years of teaching:

> It was an interesting mix, early on, between, you know, I want to do what I need to do to make sure I'm a good teacher in the eyes of my supervisor and fulfilling what the curriculum was. But there was also the sense that, even early on, there was a sense here that, if you want to try something, that's okay, "Just let me know." There was never a sense here like, "This is Tuesday, so you ought to be on Chapter 12."

The experienced teachers recall that as new teachers they had a great deal of latitude in making curriculum decisions for their own classes, but they were unsure about what to do with this freedom. They were initially inclined to follow the curriculum that had already been prepared, or to follow along with the textbook designated for a class. An experienced teacher recalls that initially she did not think to question a curriculum that was already in place:

> You know, I was so starry-eyed then, I don't know whether I questioned anything that was going on. It was a pretty established curriculum and just being able to handle that . . . so I didn't feel comfortable enough to say, "Hey, we could change this, or we could do that." That might have come with experience. I am a slow starter. I didn't even think about it then.

As this teacher notes, a change in the approach to working with the curriculum comes with experience, especially with the experience of actually having a hand in the design of the curriculum. Another experienced teacher describes the change:

> And, and now there's much less concern. . . . I know if I want to try something new, I can do it. And I would make my department chair aware or, especially if it involved getting texts or something like that. When we designed the curriculum, it involves choices, like adjusting the novels or texts that might be used. So it's kind of built into the curriculum to some extent. And if teachers want to try something new, there certainly is that prerogative for the teacher. And as a new teacher you're not really aware of all those things. But once you go through and you've helped design the curriculum, you certainly are more aware of its options. And as you have more confidence in yourself, as a teacher, you are more likely to take those chances every once in a while.

The process seems to follow this pattern: Initially, new teachers are satisfied with simply having a curriculum guide, even though they might have some doubts about elements in the established curriculum. As teachers grow and gain an understanding of the theoretical underpinnings—if there are any—of the curriculum, and see some principles for organizing the curriculum, they realize that choices are possible. Teachers are further empowered when they have contributed to the construction of the curriculum. Teachers' participation in writing curricula allows them to see the various elements in the curriculum as a unified whole. Over time, as teachers work on particular goals or work with specific literature, they can recognize some of the choices available. Here is a key distinction between experienced and new teachers. Veterans often can envision several possibilities for teaching a selected objective, whereas new teachers will see only the prescription from a curriculum guide or textbook, or see no choice at all. When new teachers lose their first option for teaching a lesson (e.g., a supplementary text is not available, the VCR is broken), they may feel a keen sense of frustration, if not panic. *Veteran teachers can draw from their recall of teaching a lesson in a variety of ways, or can draw analogies from similar lessons, and measure detailed possibilities for teaching the current lesson, even when their first option is not available.*

Personal/Physical Characteristics

In general, the experienced teachers we interviewed for this study report that at the beginning of their teaching careers they were a bit self-conscious about how their personal or physical characteristics would impede or support their efforts to do the job. There was certainly an awareness of how their youth, their size, their gender, and their demeanor might affect the way they related to students. One teacher reports that he assumed his imposing physical presence gave him an advantage:

> I had an exceptional advantage over a lot of people, in that I had some physical prowess, but I also had some accomplishments, unusual, in that they meant something to young people. Not necessarily meaning that it was that important, but, you know, as a result I had a foot in the door in terms of who was going to listen to me, in terms of whether people right off the bat listened to me.

This teacher had been a pro athlete. He recognized that his size made him a bit intimidating and that his athletic accomplishments gave him some credibility with students. In reflecting on his change as a teacher over time, he recognized that the stature adolescents accord athletes and the pretense of confidence and power his size allowed him to assume constituted a false front. Over time he came to rely on developing relationships as a means of managing students:

> I would say that the athletic prowess has given way to, after years and experience, has given way to a more empathetic tone and a more polished and controlled demeanor, and age and experience and things that allow me to still bring my large person and my maleness to the plate when a lot of students expect me to be imposing, and I got [so] as to not [let that] get that out of control as much and I think that people just appreciate the effort, and it is kind of character building and that sort of thing.

The experienced teachers report that with age and experience comes a sense of confidence, which appears to be an attitude and demeanor that becomes more important than being physically imposing. As one teacher explains:

And I think that's the difference, is the experienced teachers walk in with a confidence, with a comfortable air about them, a demeanor that says, "I know what I'm doing and I'm here to help you, and I'm going to help you get where you need to go." I think that's what it comes through, it's not really a matter of height, or physical attributes or anything like that, or dress. I think it comes down to confidence. And as I said, in my early days I walked in and I'd be hesitant or hunch or be nervous about things, and it wasn't what I was wearing. It wasn't the suit, it was my demeanor, it's, it was the attitude of, it was the lack of confidence that I, that gradually grew over time. Not the lack of confidence, but the, the hesitancy was replaced with confidence. And confidence in how I was doing something, also. And how I was approaching what we were doing.

The same teacher reports that the confidence derives in part from having a command of the subject and a clear sense of direction for what she is teaching:

And if [students] know that, that number one, you're there to help them, if they know you know the material, that you have a goal, and you're going to help them get to that goal, and you're confident, you're comfortable there, I think they can tell when you're uncomfortable. It all plays a role.

The learning process for teachers involves reflection on the meaning of experience. In the midst of the action, it is hard for beginning teachers to have an objective sense of whether their actions and decisions were right or wrong, wise or ill conceived:

When you are young, inexperienced I mean, you make good decisions, but you are not sure they are good. And with years, you made enough of those decisions that you have good feedback on, so you continue. That's in the realm of the bag of tricks. It's like I can decide the first year, I can decide to trust all of my students completely, and you know what? You get two weeks down the road and you get cheated a couple of times and you think, "Well, that's out the window; I can never trust anyone again." And that's not true at all.

This teacher's reflection recalls Mark Twain's entry in Pudd'nhead Wilson's calendar:

We should be careful to get out of an experience only the wisdom that is in it—and stop there; lest we be like the cat that sits down on a hot stove-lid. She will never sit down on a hot stove-lid again—and that is well; but also she will never sit down on a cold one anymore. (De Voto, 1976, p. 563)

Perhaps teachers need the perspective of time and distance, or reflective conversations with skillful peer coaches, to assess the efficacy and intelligence of their practices.

As was documented in the cases of Winnie and Christy in Chapter 3, the extent to which certain personal characteristics become critical issues will depend to a great extent on the meeting, or collision, of the school environment and the individual. Perhaps some beginning teachers can assume a false bravado and exude confidence. Alternatively, the experience of veteran teachers suggests that preservice teachers can develop some sense of confidence by understanding as fully as possible the nature of adolescence, by becoming as familiar as possible with the setting in which they will likely begin teaching, and by defining as completely as possible their mission as teachers of English. Again, defining a public self as a teacher requires the teacher to have many opportunities to try out the role and shape it into a comfortable form. Teachers develop confidence in making instructional, management, and interpersonal decisions by having many occasions to experience problems and challenges and having the means to work through them, especially in the company of peers and mentors.

The Struggle for Experience

The data from the surveys of preservice and practicing teachers revealed a number of significant differences between those who are just embarking on a career in teaching and those who have some experience in teaching. The recognition of these differences led us to wonder what happens to teachers over time to change them. We also wanted to know some of the specific ways in which experienced teachers are different from new teachers. If, for example, the survey results revealed that experienced teachers were more confident than beginning teachers about developing a positive relationship with students and about managing classes, how can we account for this sense of confidence? The answer, of course, is that experienced teachers have the benefit of experience. But what does experience provide? In the long run, how can we bring some of the benefits of experience to the new teachers, even before they have had any experience as teachers in their own classrooms?

We relied on responses to a set of problem-based teaching scenarios (Appendixes E and F) as a means of examining how experienced teachers have changed over the course of their careers, and as a way to probe why new teachers find it difficult to be more like experienced teachers. We constructed the scenarios around the concerns the beginning teachers identified in their initial interviews. The problems include a class management challenge, a possible parent conflict, the need for an impromptu lesson, a workload hurdle, a curriculum and subject knowledge uncertainty, an ethical question about a colleague's conduct, and a supervisor's observation. Some of the scenarios include more than one difficulty.

Here is the procedure we followed: First, we asked six first-year teachers from three different suburban high schools to write their explanations about what they would do in each situation represented in the scenarios. As an example, scenario 3 in Appendix E reads:

> The teacher arrives at his/her classroom ten minutes before 1st period class is to begin. The teacher opens his/her briefcase to discover that all the lesson materials are still at home on the kitchen table. The materials include the papers that the teacher had stayed up until 1:00 a.m. grading in order to fulfill a promise to return the papers today. The teacher does not have the transparency and the handouts that he/she was going to rely on to introduce a novel that the class would begin reading together.

The prompt asks the new teacher to "write a description of how you would react to the situation." After the beginning teacher responded, we asked him or her to identify an experienced English teacher in the same school whom he or she saw as a "very good teacher." We then approached the experienced teachers whom the first-year teachers identified, to ask them to respond to the scenarios in three ways: (1) How would you have responded to the situation during your first year of teaching? (2) How would you respond to the situation today? (3) If you notice any differences between the two responses, explain why there are these differences.

After we had collected responses from the experienced teachers, we shared with the first-year teachers the descriptions of the ways in which experienced teachers imagined their *current* responses to the situations. We then interviewed the first-year teachers about any differences they detected between their own responses and those of the experienced teachers. (The protocol for the interviews appears as Appendix J.) In these interviews, we probed with these basic questions: (1) Did you detect any differences? (2) If you detected any differences, why were the responses different? (3) If your responses are essentially the same, how do you account for the similarities? We finally asked, Why aren't you more like the veteran teacher you admire?

The final interviews were audiotaped and transcribed. We independently studied the transcripts and judged any patterns we recognized in the responses. The three of us then met to share our judgments and arrive at consensus about common themes across the set of six interviews.

There are certainly several limitations to the procedures we used for this phase of the research. First, we relied on the experienced teachers' abilities to recall accurately who they were as beginning teachers and to represent as candidly as possible how they would have handled each situation at the beginning of their teaching careers. We also had to rely on the candor of the first-year teachers in describing how they would handle each of the problems represented in the scenarios. In the interviews, we asked the first-year teachers to explain any differences they detected between themselves and the veteran teachers they recognized as "very good teachers." It would be reasonable to wonder about the first-year teachers' ability to articulate insightfully why there are differences between themselves and the experienced teachers.

We have to note one other caution. In reviewing all the responses to the scenarios and the transcripts of the interviews of the first-year teachers' analyses of the differences between themselves and their more experienced colleagues, we identified some occasions when the first-year teachers' responses to a problem seemed more judicious than the experienced teachers' responses. We must also note that two of the six first-year teachers who participated in this phase of the research were non–traditional age beginning teachers. They were individuals who had careers for a few years outside of teaching and returned to school to complete their teacher certification. Teaching was not their first professional experience, and their previous jobs had required the development of some interpersonal and problem-solving skills. We must acknowledge further that some new teachers have good instincts that guide them in acting in ways that seem characteristic of mature, experienced teachers.

Given these limitations, we detect some similarities in the responses of the first-year teachers. These similarities help us to conjecture about the benefits of experience and about how teacher training programs, schools, and mentors can help beginning teachers enjoy some of the benefits of experience. The analysis reveals that experience provides benefits that we discuss below under five categories: choices, anticipation, vision, awareness, and confidence.

Learning about Experienced Teachers

The first-year teachers note that a key difference between themselves and the experienced teachers they admire is that while the new teachers operate from a theoretical and general basis, experienced teachers can describe their proposed actions in great detail. The experienced teachers seem to be able to search memory and evaluate several *choices* they have available to them to contend with a problem. One first-year teacher describes the difference in this way:

> I'm doing these on theory and not what I have done. I haven't had this come up, so I am just kind of saying, "OK, in a perfect world, here is what I think I would try to do." And maybe that ends up being the right way if you have been teaching for a while, and that is what he has done.

This idea of the experienced teacher's options comes up again and again. In contrasting his response to a veteran teacher's response to the need to improvise a lesson, a first-year teacher makes this distinction:

> He is more specific in explaining how he would go about attempting to teach the lesson without the materials. What I just said was I would attempt to teach it without having the materials, so if it's something that I've actually spent time planning, I'll know mostly what I want to get done and how I want it to get done. So, even without those materials, I should be able to get the basic ideas through. He's got different ideas about how he's going to do that, so he's gotten more specific with his response.

The beginning teacher imagines that he would have a plan for the lesson and would be able to proceed in some fashion without the materials he had prepared for the lesson. In contrast, the veteran teachers can describe several options. One first-year teacher notes the distinction: "And again he's got a whole list of stuff and I just sort of made a blanket statement."

At least two benefits of experience are illustrated here. First, experienced teachers can recall several possibilities from past experience in the classroom. From recall, they can select an appropriate choice to fit the current situation. Experienced teachers probably also operate from a theoretical basis, having some critical framework for judging which possibilities are appropriate and which are best. But experienced teachers have more than the theory, because they have episodes from teaching experience to validate the direction that, in principle, they might be inclined to take. Experienced teachers not only have options from which to choose the current action, but they also have several contingencies from which to draw on in case the initial choice does not seem possible. Again, a first-year teacher makes this observation: "I don't have that big long list of contingencies like he does. It's more of a short list, sometimes including crayons. . . . With more experience, you are going to get a bigger list of—you get a bigger bag of tricks."

In part, the choices available to experienced teachers come from an ability to *anticipate* possible outcomes and complications. In response to the scenario that asks the teachers to imagine their reaction to a request to call a parent about the possibility of a conflict about a grade, one first-year teacher noted this distinction:

> He says, "I might mention this to my department chair in the beginning." Honestly, to do that or not do that did not even enter my thought process, really. I figured I would just handle it on my own unless it became a lot more serious problem. And he says now, "That I would inform [the department chair]. I would inform him immediately." I think I would tend to do that if it were, if the second conversation were problematic, I would. But my response is to try to do my best, attempt to keep it from being a more contentious issue.

The thought of alerting the immediate supervisor about a potential conflict with a parent over a grade did not occur to the first-year teacher as a possibility. The experienced teacher, however, drawing from recall of analogous episodes in the past, can anticipate the possibility of a parent wanting to seek out other people in the school for satisfaction regarding a grade dispute.

Another first-year teacher reflects on the veteran teacher's response to the scenario of the potentially contentious parent phone call:

> I guess you could say preemptive strike, if you will, for those kind of calls. And he [the veteran teacher] says, "In the end, I would have figured out a way to make sure the student earned a grade at least close to what the parent expected. Experience has taught me that the only practical response to the parent, to a parent that complains about grades, is to inflate his or her child's grades. Now that is what the parent is expecting. The administration sure won't back you up. One colleague told me once, 'Nobody complains about an A.' Lack of principles, you bet. But I'll make my stand for principles elsewhere." In other words, he wouldn't have trouble figuring out a way to fudge things a little bit.

Although the language is a bit disturbing, the first-year teacher talks about the veteran teacher making a "preemptive strike." The veteran anticipates some problems with the parent and projects taking some action that will prevent him from getting into trouble with a supervisor later. In this case, one would hope that the first-year teacher did not emulate the veteran entirely. It would be helpful, however, if the new teacher were able to anticipate possible ways in which the conversation with the parent might go sour and be able to ameliorate the situation before it becomes more complicated.

In response to a scenario that involves a potentially volatile conflict between two students in a classroom, the veteran teachers report that they would take quick action to remove one student from the classroom and attempt to correct her behavior. The first-year teachers, by and large, agree with this action. But experienced teachers report that they would go further. One, for example, says that he would, "depending upon various factors, involve counselor, parent, and Dean." The experienced teachers generally anticipate that the problem between two students during one class period might continue to be a problem in the future and affect the atmosphere of the class in general. The experienced teachers project that they would address the *type* of unacceptable behavior and direct students away from repeating the same type of behavior. The experienced teachers seem to be able to imagine some future possibilities beyond correcting the immediate problem.

Many of the teachers, both new and veteran, express some discomfort at the idea of facing the stress of grading a significant stack of papers to make a deadline for submitting grades. A first-year teacher begins a response this way: "Why in God's name am I in this situation?" One veteran teacher insists, "I wouldn't put myself in this situation, better planning." Most of the teachers respond that the solution to the problem would be to avoid placing oneself in the stressful circumstance. The experienced teachers would like to think that they are thoughtful enough planners to be able to anticipate the problem and avoid a pressure-packed situation.

New teachers report that it is helpful to know the underlying principles that drive the curriculum. While it is helpful to have access to curriculum guides and classroom materials, teachers also need to know why other teachers have determined that students should pursue particular goals, read particular texts, and engage in particular activities. Having an understanding of the guiding principles for the courses they teach allows teachers to make decisions that leave room for variation and creativity while remaining true to the central principles of the instruction. Scholes (1998) notes the difficulty that teachers of English have had over the years in confirming a *vision* of what they should be doing as teachers. Our interviews with new and experienced teachers reveal that having a clear vision of what they should teach and how to teach it is a powerful benefit for teachers in their day-to-day classroom operations.

The contrasting responses to the scenarios that would require teachers to improvise in the classroom reveal that experienced teachers have an easier time because they have a stronger sense of what the enterprise of teaching English is. An experienced teacher, contemplating the prospect of teaching a novel with which he was not very familiar, reports that he would prompt students to generate questions about their reading; he would then use their questions as a means of opening discussion. The teacher expresses confidence that the students' questions would be appropriate and sufficient means for beginning inquiry into the novel. A first-year teacher, by contrast, says:

> You know, it would depend on how well I knew the text. I think that if I knew the text better, I would say, "Yeah, let's, let's make

an activity that allows them to figure it out on their own." But I would want to craft it so I know where they would end up, instead of just saying, you know, "Take your own path; go off on whatever path you choose." I don't want to, like, leave them, you know, handholding down the path. But just, you know, point out some paths that you could take instead of just letting them run around all over the place and say, "Well, maybe you found something worthwhile, maybe you didn't."

This teacher uses the same "pathfinder" metaphor that Marshall, Smagorinsky, and Smith (1995) report is common among English teachers in their conceptions of how to engage students in discussions about literature. One of the first-year teachers notes that the experienced teacher advises, "Be more pro-active and constructivist about [your] understanding." Notice the contrast in the visions expressed by the two teachers: The beginning teacher wants to have a sense of command of the novel so that he can lead students down a path or paths to arrive at an understanding that he thinks is essential to the text. The experienced teacher expresses confidence that he and the students will be able to work from the students' questions and impressions as a means of constructing meaning from their reading of the text. One can imagine the stress for teachers who believe they must have a mastery of a work of literature in order to teach it. Put in a position of teaching a text they have read only once and for which they have not read supplementary material, new teachers fear they will be vulnerable to students who will pose questions that challenge the teachers' recall or understanding.

One first-year teacher quotes the veteran teacher's projection about working with students in studying a text that he was not entirely confident about teaching: "Anticipate as many questions as I could, challenge the students to find the answers on their own by asking each other, and then applaud the students for their enthusiasm and desire to learn and not get frustrated with them because they are enthusiastic." The veteran teacher goes on to say that he would "use their questions to guide the discussion and have the students pose and respond to questions." This is a possibility for instruction the first-year teacher had not thought of. She observes:

I would not have thought of that prior to October, because of my discussions with [one of my supervisors]. He's taught me about authentic discussion and questioning techniques and the fact that their questioning themselves is a good thing, and all that sort of dialogue that we had, so I wouldn't have thought of that. But now looking back, now I have that knowledge.

The new teacher here accounts for a shift in her vision of instruction that would affirm the practices her veteran colleague describes.

The responses of the first-year teachers reveal that they were not aware of some possibilities the veteran teachers knew about. Without the *awareness* of features of the school organization, of common practices among colleagues, and of traditions in the school or profession, the new teachers' choices for action were limited. In reflecting on his more experienced colleague's projection of handling a class management challenge, for example, the first-year teacher observes: "The other thing, he suggests peer mediation and also, I haven't mentioned that. Probably because I wasn't even aware that there was a peer mediation deal here. That probably accounts for most of it." Peer mediation was a resource available to help students work out conflicts, but the new teacher had not been aware of the possibility. Taking advantage of peer mediation was not a choice when the beginning teacher was not aware of the availability of the resource.

In response to the scenario in which a supervisor plans to make a formal classroom observation, a veteran teacher notes, "The Union might be contacted or consulted because formal observations should be mutually agreed upon." The first-year teacher then observes, "He—this is definitely coming from more experience and also the fact that he is a Union rep." The veteran teacher was aware and concerned that the supervisor would have certain contractual obligations. The first-year teacher assumed that if a supervisor asked to observe his class, he would have no recourse but to oblige. In reflecting on the veteran teacher's response, the first-year teacher observes, "I think the interesting thing, certainly the most outstanding difference between his answer and mine, I talked nothing about contracts and the Union and my rights as the teacher. It didn't even occur to me." Perhaps the first-year teacher would not have changed his approach even if he had been familiar with the contract language, but without an awareness of contractual obligations and his rights and limitations, he feels that he has limited choices.

In another scenario, contending with a backlog of papers that need to be graded before progress report grades can be submitted, an experienced teacher notes that he would do his best to grade as much as possible; but if the completion of all the grading were unrealistic, he would postpone some of the work until the next grading period within the same semester. Here is the first-year teacher's reaction:

> I never thought of that. I never thought of doing that. . . . I thought there was like a law about that or something. . . . I never, I just thought, as a teacher that's my job. I can't put it in another [grading period], because the students are expecting it to be on their grading period. I didn't think that that was an option. Is it an option?

In a sense, the veteran teacher was revealing a practice that many teachers probably follow but do not freely discuss. In fact, even with the revelation that a much-admired veteran teacher could contemplate postponing some of his grading, the first-year teacher has trouble reconciling this as a legitimate practice. She wonders if she would be breaking a law.

Perhaps the advantages discussed so far—choices, anticipation, vision, and awareness—all contribute to the development of *confidence*. The first-year teachers reveal that without confidence they are often inhibited in making decisions and taking the actions they feel inclined to take. This problem is most evident in the responses to two scenarios: one that invites them to intervene in a colleague's questionable behavior and a scenario about a supervisor's badly timed classroom observation.

The central conflict represented in the first of these scenarios is this: in the staff lounge, a teacher hears a colleague describe how he selects what he judges to be some of the weaker compositions from his ninth-grade class, makes transparencies of the compositions, and projects them in class for critique. One first-year teacher responds to the scenario this way:

> He's got more of a, more of an idea, you know, what's good, what's bad, and more of a place to say so. It's not my place to say it yet, I mean, I might know it might be the right way. You know, just because I think it's, you know, kind of dirty and you really shouldn't be doing it, I don't know that for a fact. I haven't tried it. You know, this person has probably tried it both ways.

First of all, the several punctuation breaks in the response reveal a hesitancy about the decision not to call the teacher on his practice. The first-year teacher suspects that "[he] might know it might be the right way." That is, he knows what the more appropriate practice would be, but he is in a position to doubt himself, because he has not validated his inclinations through experience. He continues:

> But I just don't have the experience to be a qualified, you know, judge of that. So I'd just say, "Well, okay, personally I think you're an ass but that doesn't mean you're doing it wrong," you know. I wouldn't do it, but, you know, five years from now I could be, even change my mind. It might end up being the right way to do it.

At the moment, the first-year teacher thinks it is inappropriate for a teacher to make transparencies of students' compositions and critique them in front of the rest of the class; but the new teacher has sufficient doubts because he entertains the possibility that he might discover over time that this is an effective and legitimate practice.

The doubt prevents the first-year teacher from imagining that he would intervene to question the teacher who displays and critiques the work of students. First of all, he finds it futile to try to advise a veteran about the questionable ethics of the teacher's instructional practice. He observes, "But, you know, if it's a veteran teacher especially, my personal opinion isn't going to mean squat. It's going to be, you know, 'Here's what I've done. It's worked for me so far, why should I change?'" On the other hand, the first-year teacher believes that it would be appropriate for his experienced colleague to correct his peer. He says, in reviewing the veteran teacher's response to this scenario, the fact that he has said, you know, that he would probably talk to that person, gives me the sense that, yeah, he has, or in this situation he does feel that he's got some sort of relationship with this other teacher. You know, he is allowed to make a comment on their teaching practice.

In other words, the first-year teacher recognizes that the veteran who intervenes has a rapport with his peer and has some moral authority to be able to advise him; the new teacher, however, has doubts about his own insights and wonders if he is "allowed" to intervene.

The first-year teachers also express doubts about an impending classroom observation and evaluation. The veteran teachers would be inclined to reschedule the observation, with no hesitation, if the observation were an unnecessary intrusion; or they would proceed with their lesson as originally planned. The first-year teachers wonder how they could fashion the observed lesson in a way that would impress the supervisor and protect their job status. In one first-year teacher's assessment: "I'd just be concerned about covering up my own butt. . . . Being a first-year teacher, you try to make sure everything goes as smoothly as possible with regard to observation." The first-year teachers report that they would be inclined to try to fashion the lesson to satisfy the supervisor. One teacher reports:

> If I knew that I wasn't completely prepared, and I knew that I was still going to get observed, I would plan my lesson on what I knew worked well with those kids. I wouldn't try to, like on another day, say I know fifth period doesn't like lecture, I might say, well, lecture is needed for this lesson, it's necessary and I am going to make them do it no matter what, and if it doesn't work perfect, they need to have lecture for this. But if an observer was to come, I would change it around and make it so group work was involved, so they were happy and the lesson went well and I got a good observation out of it.

The new teachers feel compelled to alter the planned lesson, if necessary, to meet some imagined criteria for judging their performance; and the criteria would be specific to the particular supervisor who observed the lesson. The veteran teachers may know the supervisors well but express little concern about how a supervisor will judge them. They express confidence that they know what they are doing, that the supervisor is aware of their competence, and that they need not perform out of the ordinary in order to satisfy some observer.

It is clear that experience equips veteran teachers with several advantages. We have discussed some obvious advantages: choices, anticipation, vision, awareness, and confidence. Our recognition of these advantages prompts an important question: If experience provides teachers with benefits that are essential to the job, how can new teachers gain some of those benefits without waiting, and perhaps stumbling, through years of experience? We discuss some of the possibilities in greater detail in the following chapters. Here we briefly review five general directions for helping new teachers speed the process of accruing the benefits of experience.

Immersion in the Experience of Teaching

First, as part of preservice training, prospective teachers should immerse themselves in real and simulated experience. Many college and university programs provide for this experience by requiring clinical observations and practicum experiences. We have learned from this study to make changes in the clinical observations for the preservice teachers we supervise. The clinical experience should include more than sitting at the back of a classroom observing classes. Clinical experiences must include actual interaction with students, both in teaching minilessons and in facilitating small-group activities. In this phase of their preparation, preservice teachers should be involved in the assessment of the learning that logically connects with any minilessons the practicing teachers design and execute. The teachers-in-training should also assess students' compositions and other products and performances, under the supervision of a cooperating teacher. These few activities should provide a more realistic glimpse of the variety and complexity of a teacher's routine.

In addition to garnering potentially valuable experiences during clinical hours in the schools, preservice teachers can practice with their peers. There is merit to structuring opportunities for preservice teachers to collaborate with peers to design units of instruction and to assess student learning. With peers as the target learners, preservice teachers should teach lessons, videotape their work, and solicit feedback to guide adjustments and improvement. These efforts contribute to the new teachers' attempts to figure out who they are supposed to be: drill sergeant or encounter group leader; distant tyrant or compassionate counselor; loud or soft; strict or lenient; fast or slow. The further along a person is in figuring out a comfortable persona, the greater the advantage when beginning student teaching.

We have also found value in engaging emerging teachers in the examination of case studies. The Harvard Business School advanced the use of case studies as a way to immerse a group in the complex world of decision making (Andrews, 1953, 1954). As we note in an earlier publication (Johannessen & McCann, 2002), the use of case studies simulates situations under controlled conditions to allow a novice to practice without facing the real risks that might be associated with the actual experience. Several worthwhile casebooks are still available and provide vivid depictions of the kind of thorny situations anyone can encounter in schools (see, for example, Small & Strzepek, 1988; Wagner & Larson, 1995: Johannessen & McCann, 2002). The examination of case studies in the relatively protected environment of the methods class can go a long way toward preparing teachers to contend with difficult situations they might encounter when the stakes might be greater and the support less apparent.

Entering the Minds of Experienced Teachers

One of the limitations of the typical clinical observation is that the teachers-in-training simply watch the outward manifestations of teachers' planning. Perhaps the more important task, and maybe the nearly impossible task, is for the preservice teacher to enter into the mind of the teacher whom he or she observes. This means having reflective conversations about the teacher's plans for a lesson and about the decisions the teacher makes during a lesson. To do this after each of perhaps one hundred hours of observation would be burdensome for the observer and for the experienced teacher. Such conversations should, however, be scheduled as an occasional and integral part of the observation and count as part of the required time spent in the schools.

Of course, to engage in a productive and meaningful reflective conversation with an experienced teacher, the teacher-in-training must be equipped with an interview protocol. Such a protocol might include an inquiry frame and a standard set of questions. Some sources such as Costa and Garmston's *Cognitive Coaching* (2002) can suggest structures for engaging practitioners in reflective conversations. The inquiry frame underlined below, for example, offers a positive presupposition: "<u>In light of your expectation to assist students in becoming better independent writers</u>, how have you planned to help them to understand a strategic process for composing?" Here are two other examples of questions to prompt conversations about the planning of lessons:

- ◆ Given that you are working with a group of students in an "accelerated" class, how have you planned to present them with appropriate challenges?
- ◆ How have you differentiated instruction to help language minority students with the literacy tasks that might present them with special challenges?

If a preservice teacher has planned carefully and has made some notes during observations, he or she might want to ask questions like the following:

- ◆ What were you thinking about when you changed from your stated plan in the middle of the lesson?
- ◆ How were you able to decide who to call on to initiate today's discussion?
- ◆ What guided your choice in forming groups and designing a structure for small-group discussion?

Without preparation, many preservice teachers would find it awkward to attempt a reflective conversation with an experienced teacher. It would be useful to practice with peers, with the university or college instructor, or with a visiting teacher in a methods class.

Instructors in methods classes routinely invite experienced teachers to visit with preservice teachers to reveal to them the reality of the school and the classroom. It is also common for the visitor to regale the initiates with stories about unruly students, blockheaded administrators, and narrow-minded colleagues. Visits from experienced teachers will be most valuable if the conversations expose the thinking processes that distinguish the experienced teacher from the neophyte. Here are examples of questions that might get such conversations started:

- What factors do you take into account as you plan a lesson?

- How do you connect several lessons into a coherent whole?

- How do you get everyone involved in the discussion of literature?

- How do you balance independent choice for students and the need to have a shared learning experience?

- How do you incorporate grammar instruction in your total language arts program?

- How do you examine social issues without proselytizing about your own political interests?

If a set of questions alone does not prompt meaningful discussion with the visiting teacher, perhaps the examination of, and reaction to, classroom scenarios or school-based case studies could help reveal the ways that experienced teachers think about instruction and decision making. Instructors for methods classes would do well to select carefully whom they invite to class and how they structure and facilitate the discussion to go beyond superficial scans of schools and to showcase the thinking processes that guide experienced practitioners.

Continuing the Conversations

Once new teachers reach the schools, it is important for them to work with experienced staff members who can serve as reliable mentors. The experienced colleagues might be the designated mentors who are part of a designed mentoring program, or informal mentors to whom the new teachers naturally gravitate. We note two cautions here. First, a school's designated mentor may not be the appropriate person with whom to work. The observation from one of the first-year teachers in the study reveals the danger: "My mentor did not want to be a mentor. She hates me; I hate her. I wanted to be with another teacher with whom I have more in common and a good teacher." Our subject defined here a dysfunctional mentoring situation. Even if a school does not match a new teacher with a compatible mentor, however, the new teacher can seek his or her own choice for the "unofficial" and more compatible mentor. This introduces the second caution: New teachers must select a mentor carefully. The study reveals several reasons why new teachers might not be retained by a school district. One common scenario sounds like the destructive situation our parents warned us about in our youth: the new teacher connected with the wrong crowd. We regret seeing instances when a veteran teacher took it upon himself or herself to accept the newcomer as an unwitting protégé whom he or she could train to be adversarial, distrustful, resistant, and cynical. Under this kind of tutelage, the new teacher turns a deaf ear to warnings from supervisors and to constructive counsel from more benevolent advisors. Polonius advises his son Laertes: "Those friends thou hast, and their adoption tried, / Grapple them to thy soul with hoops of steel." The sentiment applies to mentors: When you find good ones, bind them to your heart as long as you can.

One of the obvious benefits of mentoring is that veteran teachers know a lot about the school and about teaching. In some instances, a school's mentor program is structured to deliver that knowledge whether the newcomer is ready for it or not. While trying to avoid overwhelming the newcomer with information, the mentor can be proactive in sharing the kind of knowledge that gives the experienced teacher a distinct advantage over the new teacher. On the most basic level, the mentor can help the new teacher project the course of the school year, to recognize the ebb and flow of responsibilities. The mentor can serve a basic function by helping the new employee look forward in preparation for assemblies and special-bell schedules, for the submission of grades for progress reports, for parent-teacher conferences, and for the holidays that trigger adolescent exuberance.

Initial conversations that help new teachers look ahead to the events that mark the school calendar are all part of the experienced teachers' natural inclination to anticipate coming events. In a more significant way, mentors can help new teachers anticipate potential problems: inevitable complaints from parents, disputes about grades, stressful observations by supervisors, and possible conflicts with colleagues. Each school will have its own culture and its own concerns, but the mentor can assess and describe the potential for problems so that difficult experiences are not total surprises that leave the beginner ill-equipped to respond. In the long run, the important conversations will focus on instructional matters: what is important to teach and what are the best ways to teach. As we note in the following section, these are the conversations that should involve many colleagues: mentors, supervisors, and peers. The important point for the moment is that mentors cannot wait with an open invitation to new teachers to come see them when they need help; instead, mentors should assume that the new teachers always could use help, so they need to be proactive in sharing and inquiring.

Talking to Peers

The mentor model recognizes that the inexperienced person can benefit from the knowledge and understanding of the experienced person. At the same time, new teachers should not forget to tap the resources of their peers. We recognize that peers can be more empathetic and far less threatening than older colleagues and supervisors. No matter how supportive the mentors and supervisors would like to appear, new teachers are usually somewhat hesitant about asking questions and seeking help for fear that their appeals might be perceived as evidence of their shortcomings or failures. While conversations between peers might appear to constitute the uninformed leading the uninformed, those conversations can reveal the variety of options that each teacher alone may not have envisioned. Although conversations may initially amount to little more than venting about frustrations, the venting can be a healthy release of negative energy. As conversations develop between peers, teachers can examine a variety of approaches to teaching common concepts and skills. Peers can reveal to one another the personal approaches they take to form a positive rapport with their students. Peers might share their trepidation about an approaching observation by a supervisor and learn from one another how to form a positive working relationship with a department chair or administrator. As with the work with mentors, the conversations with peers expose new teachers to the variety of choices they have for approaching lessons, for creating a positive learning environment, and for developing strong relationships with colleagues. Again, a factor that distinguishes the experienced teachers from the new teachers is that experience furnishes veterans with a repertoire of choices for delivering instruction and for working with students, parents, and colleagues.

Working with Supervisors

Supervisors play an important role in the induction of new teachers. A common experience for new teachers is a meeting with the supervisor, who shows the newcomer his or her room (or rooms, in some cases) and who hands the new faculty member the textbooks that are the curricular basis for the assigned classes. In other cases, the supervisor hands the new teacher an unwieldy curriculum guide that provides more than abundant information and materials. Neither experience is especially helpful. While one approach provides lots of freedom, it also provides little guidance. The other approach provides apparent support, but it also overwhelms and handcuffs the beginning teacher. An alternative to these extremes is for a supervisor (or mentor or lead teacher) to sit down with the beginner to explain the general principles that governed the design of the curriculum. The new teacher will need to have some initial answers to these questions: What is really important to teach? What proficiencies should I be able to see in my students by the end of a term? Is it important to cover a lot of material? Is it more important to influence a deep understanding of a limited number of key concepts? What will students be expected to know as they transition to the next grade? Knowing the underlying principles for the design of the curriculum empowers the new teacher and allows for some creative flexibility: as long as the teacher remains true to the basic principles, it is possible to explore a variety of creative ways to deliver instruction.

Supervisors also have a responsibility to support the induction of the new teacher into a larger professional community. If a supervisor provides no other encouragement, he or she needs to prompt the new teacher to participate in school-sponsored professional development activities and to connect with other staff to become part of the social and intellectual fabric of the school. In a broader sense, supervisors would do well to remind new teachers of the benefits of membership in professional organizations like NCTE and its affiliates and to participate in the professional meetings they sponsor. Even if new teachers cannot travel to conferences, reading professional journals and sharing their contents with colleagues is part of the professional life of those teachers who plan to continue to grow and to remain in teaching. The connection to the larger professional community affirms the importance of the mission of schools and of particular disciplines and underscores the critical role that teachers play.

Steps toward Helping Beginning Teachers

Support for Teacher Retention

After forty-four interviews with the new and experienced teachers in this study, we were struck by the varied and haphazard paths that people have followed in becoming high school English teachers. How one develops as a teacher is subject to many factors: the choice of college or university where one trains, the particular methods classes one takes and the philosophical bent and theoretical frame of the instructors one encounters, the school placement for completing clinical experiences, the match with a cooperating teacher and university supervisor, and finally the culture of the school and the department where one begins the first job. Obviously the nature and quality of the combined experiences will be remarkably varied and subject to innumerable chance factors. We marvel that many teachers manage to thrive after completing such a curious course of development.

The purpose of this and the next chapter is to suggest ways to make the path to developing as an English teacher less haphazard and more consistent and supportive. While intuition and experience might suggest hundreds of ways to help a new teacher grow and thrive, we limit our recommendations to those that have an apparent connection to the beginning teachers' expressed concerns. We also encourage practices that could influence new teachers to become, as quickly as possible, more like the experienced teachers we interviewed. We recognize that our recommendations cover topics that could invite book-length discussions. We review the recommendations briefly, realizing that other authorities can provide advice about the procedural details for accomplishing a plan of action. Although we recommend that schools provide supportive induction and mentoring programs, for example, the reader can refer to the many published models for details on how to implement such programs.

A review of the concerns of beginning teachers provides some direction for taking action to ease the induction into teaching and to encourage teacher retention. While some solutions may seem obvious, they may not be readily available. If teachers leave because of low salaries, for example, the obvious response would be to increase salaries. In general, and as educators who have sometimes labored in systems that paid paltry salaries, we affirm the wisdom of salary increases as incentives to stay in teaching; however, we also recognize that new teachers, their university professors, or individual administrators cannot by fiat designate a restructured salary schedule for teachers. Perhaps federal, state, and district policymakers can work strategically over a number of years to change the way in which teachers are compensated. In the meantime, prospective teachers continue to train and teachers continue to teach.

We propose here some of the available actions that teacher preparation programs and schools can take to improve the lot of beginning teachers and equip them to have a better chance of remaining in the profession. While we discuss the actions that colleges and universities and high schools can take separately, we also highlight some initiatives that colleges and universities can take in *partnership* with the schools.

Finally, and perhaps most important, we recommend some steps that beginning teachers can take to help themselves. We recognize that school district policies and settings can vary widely, and teacher preparation programs can be drastically different. In large university programs, the methods classes can be vastly different, depending on the professor in charge. There are many factors that new teachers cannot control, but in most circumstances there are actions that teachers can take to help themselves. We emphasize a discussion of the means new teachers can take to form positive relationships with the significant agents in their teaching experience—the students, their parents, colleagues, and supervisors. We also offer advice about managing time and an unwieldy workload, about developing the knowledge of subject and curriculum, about protecting autonomy, and about grading student performances.

Ingersoll (2002) reports that approximately half of those teachers who leave teaching cite "job dissatisfaction" and a "desire to pursue a better job" as the reasons for leaving. Ingersoll further notes:

> Those who depart because of job dissatisfaction most often cite low salaries, lack of support from the school administration, lack of student motivation, student discipline problems, and lack of teacher influence over decision making as the causes of their leaving. (p. 26)

Ingersoll's analysis of survey data lists the several individual factors that teachers cite as reasons for leaving the profession. Of course, many factors may work together to influence a teacher to leave or to stay in teaching. If a teacher were earning a modest salary but enjoying the job tremendously, for example, it is unlikely that the teacher would leave. On the other hand, if a teacher were earning very little while experiencing frustrations with unmotivated students and unsupportive supervisors, the teacher is not likely to tolerate the combination of unsatisfactory circumstances. In sum, schools should look to improve as many conditions as possible to diminish frustration and support the possibility of teacher satisfaction.

What Schools Can Do to Help

If one grants that school leaders are not in a position to guarantee lucrative contracts, pristine working conditions, and model students, there are still a number of positive steps that decision makers in schools can take to increase the extent of teachers' job satisfaction and enhance the likelihood that they will remain on the job. We propose eight actions that leaders can take in any school to support the retention of beginning teachers.

1. Give the new teacher a reasonable teaching assignment, with few preparations and little movement among classrooms. We have met a high school English teacher who taught five different preparations in five different locations in the school, including one class in the balcony above the swimming pool. We fear that some readers can report even worse teaching scenarios. Obviously, such a teaching assignment will impose debilitating fatigue and amplify frustration. Ideally, new teachers should have only a couple of manageable preparations, with a minimum of movement from classroom to classroom. Some battle-hardened old-timers may continue to embrace the pioneer adage that if the difficult conditions don't kill you, they will make you stronger. But though the idea that enduring trials early in a teacher's career will prepare him or her to triumph over difficulties in the future seems intuitively sensible, this kind of survival-of-the-fittest rationale for allowing new teachers to suffer unnecessarily has no place in a climate of teacher shortages, nor in any school culture that can provide more compassionate means for inducting a teacher into the profession.

It is hard enough as a novice to attend to the many details of the job without complicating the situation further with multiple preparations and classroom moves. The exaggerated self-consciousness that anyone new to a job is likely to experience inhibits flexibility and easy decision making. If new teachers are fielding requests for washroom use, attending to questions about homework, handling current lessons, and attempting lesson adjustments at the same time they are worrying about moving themselves and materials to another side of the building, their performances are likely to be impaired. The circumstances in each building and each department will dictate to a large extent the constraints for making teacher assignments, and it is impossible to insist on a firm limit for assigning a teacher's class load. At the same time, administrators can be guided by a general principle: For the new teacher, keep the preparations to a minimum, and make the movements manageable.

2. Plan for formal and informal mentoring, without encumbering the new teacher with additional time commitments and without imposing an inappropriate partner on the novice. Some consultants who make their living training mentors report that it is better for a school to have no mentor program at all than to have a bad mentor program. Earlier in this report, we cite a first-year teacher who expresses frustration with her school's mentoring program, which imposes threats and penalties if the new teachers do not participate in Friday afternoon group "mentoring" sessions. The teacher observes, "The mentoring program at this school would drive people away from teaching." One of the group mentoring activities featured an administrator reading aloud several pages from the student discipline policy. We will not presume to describe the ideal mentor program here. Obviously, however, a model mentoring program would do the opposite of the practices this first-year teacher reports.

Several sources can guide schools in devising a mentor program (see, for example, Lipton, Wellman, and Humbard [2003] and Villani [2002]). We can imagine many variations on mentoring, but we also think that a meaningful program would include the following features: (1) careful selection and training of the mentors, including training in sound communication and peer coaching techniques, (2) attention to the actual expressed concerns of beginning teachers, (3) special consideration for the inevitable exhaustion and decline that teachers experience after the first nine to ten weeks of school, (4) a program of regularly scheduled contacts between the new teacher and the mentor, and (5) assistance in acclimating the new teacher to the school community. Other suggestions like the ones listed in items 3 and 4 below would also be appropriate elements in a school's mentoring program.

3. Plan for an induction process, with an orientation; inservice training in working with the curriculum; and ongoing, relevant staff development opportunities. Most schools provide some sort of orientation for new staff. The training should go beyond a set of talking heads enumerating the rules, policies, and procedures for the school. Orientation should include careful attention to the questions of the new staff. It would be useful to project for the new staff members the cycle of the school year to help them anticipate difficult times and recognize that it is normal and natural to feel fatigue and some frustration.

It seems to make intuitive sense to provide new teachers with detailed curriculum guides and abundant instructional materials. But new teachers benefit especially from sitting down with someone who can help them discover the underlying principles that have guided the development of the curriculum. When teachers understand the principles that drive the curriculum, they become empowered to make decisions, adjust existing materials and activities to fit their particular teaching situations, and unleash some creative energies. An orientation to a particular school and to the professional world of teaching is not the experience of a single day. A meaningful staff development program would support the new teacher's professional growth and convey the idea that teaching is a craft that school staff take seriously.

4. Support a network of collegial contacts between the new teacher and peers, veteran staff, and external resource persons. Most schools understand the induction of new teachers as a process of having older, more experienced people imparting their wisdom. The word *mentor* conjures the image of a wizened master guiding the novice. There is certainly value in having mentors and supervisors offer guidance and advice. But the new teacher can benefit from having a broad network of contacts, in and out of the school. The various contacts in the new teacher's life can serve the many needs he or she will inevitably have. Supervisors have the official responsibility of providing guidance and assistance. One can well imagine, however, that a new teacher might hesitate to report troubles to a supervisor for fear that the admission of a need for help might negatively influence an evaluation of the teacher's job performance. In their design of mentoring programs, many schools are careful to distinguish the role of mentor as one with no evaluation responsibilities. If the mentor is someone the new teacher admires and respects as a professional authority, however, it is natural for the new teacher to feel hesitant about admitting failures and describing difficulties to the mentor. Sometimes a new teacher needs to vent frustrations or tell the story of doubts and challenges to an objective or disinterested other. A sympathetic listener might be another first-year teacher, a friend, a former classmate or instructor, or a family member. As experience grows and opportunities expand, a teacher will make contacts with other teachers from other schools.

We refer again to the comment of a first-year teacher who was the focus of one of our case studies. She noted that the conversations with a university researcher were "therapeutic." Her depiction of the series of interviews was enlightening for us. We thought of her participation in the study as a service to *us*, not imagining that our seeking information from her would also serve her needs. In the interviews, the researcher inquired about the teacher's experience, conveying a genuine sense of interest in the nature of the teacher's first year in the profession. The researcher was not in a position to judge the teacher or recommend changes. The researcher simply prompted the teacher to tell the story about her experience. It would be a rare school that actually planned for someone to perform a role similar to the one the university researcher performed, but we see great potential in having someone perform this role. In the end, the new teacher would have several contacts, each serving a separate function: supervisor, mentor, peers, veteran colleagues, friends, former college classmates and instructors, and objective listener/observer.

5. Follow a supportive evaluation plan that focuses on professional development and discourages punitive approaches to teacher evaluation. We begin with the assumption that a teacher evaluation plan will be in place in a school to promote the professional development of the certificated staff. Realistically, evaluation plans do provide a framework for making decisions about continued employment. At the same time, the plan should structure procedures for guiding and encouraging a teacher in his or her professional development.

If the leaders in a school expect the teacher evaluation plan to be a means for promoting teachers' growth, then one can draw parallels to other instructional plans. A lesson that simply assigns learners a task and then assesses their competence in executing the task does not include steps for showing how to complete the task successfully. Similarly, a teacher evaluation plan that provides only for the assessment of the observed performance of the teacher, without the pre- and postobservation conferences that could facilitate reflection and allow the teacher to select corrective steps to improve performance and enhance instruction, is not likely to promote professional growth.

Supervisors should convey explicitly that the goal of the evaluation plan is to promote growth. Again, one can draw a parallel to a teacher relating to students in a classroom. We recommend that teachers announce to students their hope and intention of helping students learn an important subject. Similarly, supervisors should acknowledge that while a particular teaching assignment might be tough, the supervisor intends to provide assistance and fully expects the teacher to do a good job. Perhaps a sports analogy is also appropriate here. Imagine two baseball managers each sending a relief pitcher into a crucial game when runners are in scoring position and the game is on the line. One manager gives the pitcher the ball with this instruction: "Don't goof up!" The second manager tells the relief pitcher: "You have the support of the team behind you. We have confidence that you can do the job. Now go get 'em!" We would like to see supervisors of new teachers be more like the second manager.

6. Monitor a new teacher's experiences through formal and informal observations and through a series of professional conversations. We have experienced working in schools where the supervisors made cursory observations once or twice a year. It is hard to imagine that a supervisor can have a strong sense of a teacher's performance and experience on the basis of a couple of observations. Whether or not the observations are a formal procedure as part of a teacher evaluation plan, having supervisors and mentors observe teachers on separate occasions and engage in professional conversations with the teachers about the observations would support growth. We must grant that the observations will be worthwhile as formative assessments only if everyone involved proceeds in a spirit of coaching and support. The observations would need to be planned and accompanied by reflective conversations. Under this model, the teacher being observed would work with the observers to identify the focus of the observations and to specify the data for the observers to collect and the means for collecting them. The teacher and the supervisor would meet to discuss the meaning and significance of the data.

7. Take proactive measures to help new teachers anticipate crises that might confront them in school and explore and assess pos-

sible courses of action to meet each challenge. Inevitably, the new teacher will encounter some difficulties: an unruly class, an angry parent, a tough evaluation, a curriculum conundrum. An experienced teacher can help a new colleague predict the possibilities. It would be worthwhile for a supervisor, mentor, or peer coach to help the new teacher anticipate tough situations and devise some problem-solving strategies for contending with them. Of course, each challenging situation will have its own nuances and unique complications, but one can usually draw on the experience of one problem-solving situation to explore options in responding to a new challenge. Often problems and their solutions are specific to a particular school. Perhaps, for example, an especially intrusive and powerful group of band boosters triggers a proliferation of fund-raising that spills over into instructional time. This problem might be unique to a particular school; the appropriate steps for responding to the problem might be unique to the school as well. While a new teacher might not face a specific projected problem, the discussion of possibilities does train a person to think about ways to solve problems within a particular organization and to realize that there are resources available to provide help.

8. To convey an expectation that each teacher is connected to a larger community of education professionals, encourage new teachers to engage in professional activities and to develop contacts outside the school. The staff in some schools convey the expectation that teachers will be involved in professional activities outside of school. Joining an organization like NCTE or one of its affiliates does confirm that a teacher is making a professional commitment. Being part of a network of teachers across a state or across the country suggests that teachers see themselves as professional educators who are committed to growing as teachers and learning more about the field of knowledge.

We judge that the teachers who are most likely to remain in teaching beyond their induction years have a keen interest in developing their knowledge and skills as teachers. They can talk about how they have grown over the course of their initial year, and they can account for the factors that have helped them to grow. In some schools, the wealth of talented, positive people in the building serve as models and provide many immediate learning resources. In schools with smaller faculties and more limited resources, or in schools where the culture does not elevate the importance of professional involvement, it is all the more critical that new teachers establish professional links outside of the school. In some instances, the only substantive dialogue a teacher has will be with another English teacher several states away, or through the reading of and responses to professional journals. Schools need to support the effort and recognize that a teacher's attendance at a conference or investment in a membership is not a superfluous lark but an essential part of professional development.

Steps That Teacher Education Programs Might Take

Teacher training programs draw from the experience of their instructors, from the research about current best practices, and from scans of school environments to project the needs of new teachers and plan experiences that will prepare them for the world of teaching. Teacher training programs need to be sensitive to the reported concerns and frustrations of new teachers as well as attentive to the typical practices of skilled experienced teachers in order to model how to plan, manage, and relate. Of course, methods classes will guide prospective teachers in thinking about the subject and the delivery of instruction. Also part of the training should be attention to helping preservice teachers begin to develop a teacher persona, and attention to anticipating the reality of the life of teaching.

1. Provide opportunities to help prospective teachers develop problem-solving skills that will equip them to contend with the kind of conflicts and problems they will likely face in school, and explore and assess possible courses of action to meet each challenge. We have found that for the beginning teacher, the actual experience of teaching is often very different from their expectations for teaching. If new teachers are pleasantly surprised that their students are bright, courteous, and cooperative, that is one thing; if they expect respect, admiration, and tangible success but face resentment, apathy, and doubt, however, they will experience frustration. It would be worthwhile, as part of the teacher training program, for prospective teachers to grapple together with some of the difficulties they might encounter on the job: e.g., censorship challenges, curricular inconsistencies, literacy lapses, assessment dilemmas, and classroom management difficulties.

An obvious answer to the problem of having unrealistic expectations about teaching is to get prospective teachers into schools and into classrooms. The limitation to many clinical experiences, however, is that the observer sees only the surface reality. Someone needs to walk in the teacher's shoes to know when a supervisor's visit is dismaying or when a student's failure is frustrating. It is hard to re-create the environment the classroom teacher experiences from day to day. To a certain extent, the use of case studies simulates the experience of working through some of the troublesome episodes new teachers might encounter. The process of consulting with peers about measuring the benefits and harms that may result from each choice one makes as a teacher gives some insight into daily life in the classroom. Case studies have been used to much advantage in many university programs, and some good casebooks are available for use with the prospective English teacher: Johannessen and McCann (2002), Wagner and Larson (1995), and Small and Strzepek (1988). Without much difficulty, instructors or their teachers-in-training can create their own cases to help preservice teachers anticipate the experience of the first years of teaching.

2. Maintain contacts with new teachers after they have graduated and received their teaching certificates. New teachers often maintain informal contacts with classmates and instructors from their teacher training programs. In some instances, graduates relied on peers and instructors for support and guidance when they were in school. An abrupt break from those contacts can be a significant loss for someone who is attempting to find his or her way in a new profession.

When college or university personnel maintain contact with their graduates as the new teachers begin teaching, they serve an important role. First, they convey to graduates that the institution remains invested in the new teachers' success. If a college or university follows a graduate at the start of his or her teaching career, the implied message is that what you do as a teacher is so important that the university is going to follow you as you begin in the profession.

A college or university contact serves another important function. If the contact is not evaluating or directing the new teacher, the conversations can be "therapeutic" because the contact inquires about the new teacher's experience, needs, and well-being. The university representative can perform a role that is rarely provided in schools: sympathetic, nonjudgmental listener.

3. Rely on practicing teachers to talk with preservice teachers about the experienced teachers' approaches to forming strong relationships with students, colleagues, and parents and about their approaches to planning and managing instruction. We have found that new teachers feel frustration in part because their actual teaching experience is very different from their anticipation of the experience. Veteran teachers can help to dispel misconceptions and test assumptions. This does not mean regaling methods classes with horror stories about the worst classes they have ever experienced. On the contrary, veteran teachers can describe how they develop a positive rapport with students, how they work constructively with parents, and how they form strong relationships with supervisors and peers. Visiting veteran teachers can also reveal how they plan strategically for instruction and how they assess students' performances. It would be helpful to invite visiting teachers to join methods classes to think through problem scenarios or cases and reveal problem-solving processes and to demonstrate how specific approaches might be unique to particular school settings.

4. Frequently and explicitly link theory and research about teaching to real-world practical problems that novices will likely face. While it is critical for preservice teachers to have a grasp of the theory that guides planning and practice, it is also important to be familiar with specific "real world" problems that might challenge teachers to remain true to a theoretical model for instruction. Some worthwhile casebooks (Johannessen & McCann,

2002; Wagner & Larson, 1995; Small & Strzepek, 1988) are available to help teachers apply their theoretical notions to challenges typically encountered in schools. Even without casebooks, methods instructors can structure experiences to ask preservice teachers to expand their thinking about proposed practices. How, for example, would a teacher adapt lessons to address the needs of a group of students with various learning disabilities? How would a teacher alter a unit of instruction when most of the students in his or her classes are second language learners?

New teachers in this study noted that one distinction in the way they and veteran teachers responded to hypothetical teaching challenges is that the new teachers knew how to respond in principle, but the experienced teachers could describe a set of contingencies for acting in a given situation. The apparent benefit of experience is that a teacher has recall of several related episodes to guide him or her in making decisions, and the veteran teacher can select from several possibilities in devising a detailed plan of action.

Steps That Colleges/Universities and High Schools Can Take Together

Too often, colleges, universities, and the high schools in their region operate as a loose partnership by placing student teachers and providing for clinical observations. Each party has a significant role to play in the development and retention of a beginning teacher. An awareness of the roles they can play and how they can work together should serve the interests of the emerging teacher. There are many possibilities for working in tandem. We offer five suggestions.

1. Provide preservice teachers with *numerous occasions* to assume the role of teacher: among peers, in schools, in various community settings. This requires the establishment of networks and partnerships to provide the occasions when novice teachers can immerse themselves in a teacher role and define their personas. We have reported that a notable challenge for new teachers is the

attempt to define for themselves their teacher persona. In a sense, growth in becoming a teacher is a matter of trial and error. Every day, teachers try out their public persona (i.e., rigid or flexible, tough or easy, distant or friendly, etc.) and make adjustments to become ultimately who they are. For many new teachers, their first time alone in front of a class during student teaching is the first time they have assumed the role of teacher in any form. College and university programs can structure numerous formal and informal occasions for preservice teachers to function in the role of teacher. These occasions might include teaching lessons to classmates, serving as volunteer tutors, or teaching lessons as part of clinical experiences.

We also hope that new teachers will begin their jobs with a fairly realistic picture of what teaching is all about. Colleges and universities can work with the schools where they place preservice teachers for clinical experiences to schedule occasions when the teacher-in-training can experience what practicing teachers experience: interacting with students individually, in small groups, and in large groups; planning lessons and helping with assessments; engaging in professional conversations about instructional and organizational issues. The high schools would have to be open to allowing the preservice teacher to enter into a partnership with cooperating personnel, and the colleges and universities would have to convey to the schools their purpose and expectations for such experiences.

2. Match student teachers with nurturing school environments in which teacher induction and mentoring programs are in place. The placement of student teachers sometimes suffers from internal and external politics. It is not uncommon for a university's English department to have the responsibility of training a candidate to teach English, but it is often an education department's charge to place the student teacher in a school. The two departments may not share a common vision for the best way to prepare a candidate for teaching. In some instances, the cooperating high school teacher's only qualifications to work with the student teacher is that he or she has a full schedule of English classes and a willingness to turn them over to a student teacher. The system seems rather haphazard.

We believe that student teachers have the best chance to develop a desire to continue as teachers when the college or university carefully places the prospective teachers with experienced teachers who are prepared to work with them. It will take time for a college or university to identify the particular cooperating teachers and the particular schools that can extend the candidates' training in a way that is reliable and consistent with the substance and spirit of the preservice training. Developing the network of potential cooperating teachers and placement locations will take time and require some stability and sense of vision on the part of the teacher training program. Over time the college or university supervisors will know where student teachers will most likely have positive experiences and thus can provide cooperating teachers with some training in the expectations and direction of the training program.

We would like to see new teachers get off to a great start in schools that have consciously provided for the induction and support of new employees. For the sake of the students, and for the sake of emerging teachers, it makes good sense for schools to treat student teachers in a way that is similar to the way they treat new employees. The college or university programs should look for cooperating schools that offer a strategic induction process, helping the student teacher to become familiar with the culture of the school, the expectations for performance, the available resources, and even the physical layout of the building. Presumably the cooperating teacher will serve the student teacher as mentor, but it would also be helpful if the cooperating teacher were the product of the school's mentoring program and had received mentor training.

Surveys of student teachers and reports from supervisors will inform colleges and universities about which schools and cooperating teachers supported the prospective teachers' development and which schools and cooperating teachers inhibited development. Over time, patterns will emerge to give a teacher training program direction in the productive partnerships they can cultivate and to identify the schools that still need to grow into supportive systems.

3. Ensure that clinical and student teaching experiences provide opportunities for novice teachers to develop problem-solving skills that will enable them to contend with the kind of challenges they will likely encounter in their teaching. Often colleges and universities require prospective teachers to observe for dozens of hours in schools. Too often the observations amount only to sitting in the back of a classroom and watching the lesson. The observer who sees a lesson can infer some of the thinking that produced the lesson or influenced a teacher's decisions during the lesson. It would be more useful, however, to accompany each observation with a conversation between the classroom teacher and the observer. An established framework for the conversation would guide the preservice teacher in inquiring about how the teacher conceived of the lesson and made decisions about students and procedures during the lesson.

The new teacher might also probe the cooperating teachers to learn about the critical educational issues in the local schools. What challenges predominantly occupy the thoughts and efforts of the staff? Has the school faced any controversy? In each case, how did the staff of the school think about the challenges and derive strategies for working through any difficulties?

Professional conversations will be possible only if the colleges and universities convey to the high schools that they expect their teacher candidates to engage staff in dialogue about the profession and about the local school. The partnership would allow prospective teachers to enter the minds of experienced teachers to gain some insight into how to make instructional and other professional decisions.

4. Maintain a regular dialogue that exposes the college or university to the current students and curricula in the high schools and that exposes the schools to advances in theory, research, and best practices. We hear complaints that the important research coming out of colleges and universities takes years to affect practice in the schools. We also hear complaints that the people who train prospective teachers are not aware of the daunting challenges teachers face in contemporary classrooms and that the training assumes, unrealistically, that current theory will have a happy match in current classrooms. Obviously, the colleges and universities and the high schools will need to find reciprocal means for sharing the directions suggested by current research and the needs and challenges faced by schools. Again, the goal of informing both sides of the partnership will require that key agents from the schools and from the colleges and universities meet regularly to talk about needs and vision.

In some instances, the sharing occurs casually as teachers continue graduate studies and as the university or college supervisors interact with the schools. The sharing can take a more purposeful form if school personnel were to meet with college or university staff to plan together for staff development. It is not uncommon for college and university instructors to serve as staff development consultants in schools; it makes good sense to draw on the expertise of scholars from a local college or university. The sharing is likely to be most useful to teachers when the consultant plans with the school personnel to provide training and experiences that are actually connected to the expressed needs in the school.

College and university instructors always gain from having an awareness of students today and of the classrooms where they spend much of their time. One way to maintain awareness of contemporary high schools is to enter the schools to collect data to support research or to assist classroom teachers with their own action research projects.

5. Complete long-term, strategic follow-up to track the development of novice teachers after they have left their college/university training. Many colleges and universities can cite the figures to show how many of their graduates found gainful employment in their fields of preparation after graduation. Less often can colleges and universities report how many of their graduates remained teachers beyond their first year of teaching or account for elements in their training and work experience that had a significant influence on the teachers' leaving or remaining in the profession.

Schools could work with colleges and universities in reporting how many graduates the schools hired and help the teachers report to their teacher training programs the nature of their development and experience. Again, through surveys and interviews, colleges and universities can learn how well their graduates were prepared to begin teaching and discover what new teachers perceive as the elements that could have helped them if they had been available.

Guiding New Teachers to Help Themselves

Several texts are available to guide beginning teachers through-out the first days and first year of teaching. At professional conferences, we have heard beginning teachers sing the praises of Wong and Wong (1999) and others (e.g., Kellough, 1999; Kottler, Kottler, & Kottler, 1998; Rominger, Packard, & Elkin, 2001), testifying that these texts helped them survive the very difficult beginning days of a teaching career. We don't know whether these texts were assigned reading during methods classes or if the new teachers discovered them on their own. We cannot deny that many teachers have found the texts useful. We view the initiation into the profession of teaching in a way that seems to be a bit differ-ent from the views implied by the advice offered in these and other texts. Simply put, we focus less on strategies for control-ling students and surviving induction, emphasizing instead the behaviors that will cultivate positive relationships—with students, with parents, and with colleagues, including supervisors.

We also discuss here some of the pragmatic aspects of grow-ing into a competent teacher who enjoys the job. We suggest how to handle the workload, how to grow in knowledge of subject, and how to protect one's autonomy. The list of contrasts between the practices of the beginning teachers and the practices of the experienced teachers we interviewed has guided the formulation of our recommendations. We suggest practices that would en-courage relatively inexperienced teachers to do what accomplished veteran teachers actually do. The list of suggestions is a fairly long one. We have categorized the suggestions under the areas of concerns expressed by beginning teachers; we have drawn the advice from the practices of the experienced teachers and from the coping strategies of the beginning teachers who show hope for continuing in the profession. Ultimately, we hope that teacher educators find the suggestions useful in guiding beginning teachers to help themselves. In some school environments, beginning teachers will have to rely most often on their own resolve and initiative to make bad situations better. In all schools, from time to time, individual teachers will have to rely solely on their own actions to solve problems, plan for the future, and grow as professionals.

Relationships with Students

Beginning teachers are likely to be concerned about the various relationships they will form as part of their life in a school. Of the important relationships that will develop, none is more important than the relationship new teachers will form with students, the people with whom the new teachers will spend the greatest part of the working day and the people on whom the newcomer will have the greatest impact. It is critical, then, that beginning teachers get this part of their teaching life right. Understandably, some beginners will be preoccupied with how to manage or control their classes. Many veteran teachers and guides to beginning teaching can describe effective strategies for controlling students. If a teacher emphasizes the control of students, the task is fairly simple because teachers have the advantage of being able to impose many possible punitive consequences; but while controlling students through the exercise of rewards and punishments will accomplish the desired end, the rapport with a class declines, and students will comply and cooperate only because they are coerced. In contrast, we emphasize here steps toward forming the kind of positive relationships from which respect, order, and productivity derive.

In his novel *God Bless You, Mr. Rosewater* (1965), Kurt Vonnegut invents the character Eliot Rosewater, who imagines greeting newborns at the local hospital with this message:

> Hello, babies. Welcome to Earth. It's hot in the summer and cold in the winter. It's round and wet and crowded. At the outside,

babies, you've got about a hundred years here. There's only one rule that I know of, babies: "Goddammit, you've got to be kind." (p. 110)

Rosewater's precept seems to be a universal rule, and all educators would do well to let the rule guide their daily interactions with adolescents. Of course, adolescents will pose challenges. In his memoir about beginning his teaching career in rural Kentucky, Jesse Stuart (1970) recalls that he earned the respect of his students and other members of the community by fighting and conquering Guy Hawkins, the biggest and toughest boy in the school. The residual bloodstains on the wooden floor of the Lonesome Valley schoolhouse served as a reminder to Guy Hawkins and his classmates that Mr. Stuart was in command. In a way, Jesse Stuart's actions reflect beginning teachers' greatest fear; his teaching style is an exaggeration of a model for managing the classroom. As we have noted, some guides for the beginning teacher emphasize the importance of laying down the rules and summoning the shadow of retribution for failure to comply. In contrast, experienced teachers note a different approach that has evolved for them as they have grown as professional educators.

Unlike the novice, most experienced teachers will *not* be preoccupied with imposing order on their classes. They do not begin the school year with this message:

> Good morning, children. I am Mr. Stewart. You will notice that at the front of the room I have posted fifteen rules for classroom behavior. To your left you will see an additional five rules for homework completion. Above the computer you will find seven rules for the use of technology. The first violation of any of the rules for classroom behavior will earn you a verbal reprimand; the second violation will result in a detention; the third violation will mean a trip to the dean's office.

Instead, students are more likely to hear this from an experienced teacher:

> I am Ms. Bonnacouer. This year we are going to study contemporary literature. I can't wait to get into some of the very interesting units with you. I know that some of you might have a little

difficulty at first, but experience tells me that you are all very capable and you will all do well in this class. I want to reassure you that I am here to help you. I will be available regularly before and after school to provide whatever assistance I can.

In addition, the experienced teacher is more likely to engage the students in a conversation about the goals they all have for the class and for themselves. There will be a bit of negotiation about how the teacher will run the class and set the instructional goals for the students. Although this may seem like a touchy-feely practice right out of the sixties, experienced teachers report that they actually do this sort of thing, and there are practical reasons for acting this way. First, a teacher is more likely to be successful in managing adolescents if he or she develops a positive rapport with them. This rapport is most likely to emerge when students know that the teacher has confidence in their ability to learn what the teacher is prepared to teach, is deeply interested and excited about the subject, understands students' possible fears and reservations, and is willing to support students in overcoming difficulties. In addition, as noted earlier, the teacher will want to begin planning instruction by finding out what students already know, what interests them, and who they are. As Bloom (1982), Ausubel (2000), and Rumelhart (1980) suggest, it makes good strategic sense to learn much about students; that knowledge includes learning something about the aspects of their personal lives that influence how they construct meaning from the activities in the classroom. This means learning more about them than what prerequisite academic skills students bring to the immediate classroom tasks. It is worthwhile knowing whether students have traveled the world or have never left their neighborhood, if students have extensive home libraries or have nothing to read at home beyond mail order catalogs and textbooks, if students live in safe, luxurious surroundings or dwell in impoverished homes where the threat of violence, disease, and personal loss looms every day.

In short, relying on the advice of Eliot Rosewater and avoiding Jesse Stuart's example, teachers would do well to try always to be kind and attempt to learn all they can about the students entrusted to their care. Teachers should express the expectation that students will succeed and convey some interest and excitement about the subject they teach. Teachers set a positive tone when they announce a willingness to help the students who struggle to learn the concepts of the subject. Here, then, in summary fashion, are our suggestions for building strong positive relationships with students:

Forming Relationships with Students

- ◆ Cultivate a welcome feeling and tone in your class.

- ◆ Indicate that you expect all students to achieve in your class.

- ◆ Announce that it is your hope and intention to support the students' achievement.

- ◆ Indicate that you will be available to help students outside of class time and beyond the regular school day.

- ◆ Keep your list of classroom rules short, and don't make the discussion of rules the first topic on your agenda.

- ◆ Convey the attitude that the subject you teach and the work the students do are vitally important.

- ◆ Find out over time who your students are: their talents, their interests, their activities, their challenges, and their concerns.

- ◆ Recognize your own tolerance level and know what distracts your students; don't react to students' behavior by guessing what other teachers would do.

- ◆ Respond quickly to correct misbehavior, without ridicule and without attacking the person.

- ◆ Operate with reasonable flexibility, recognizing that students often take several challenging classes in one semester and may have co-curricular, employment, and family obligations.

Relationships with Parents

For the most part, parents put their trust in schools and teachers and assume that educators know what they are doing and are acting in the best interest of the children in their care. In some schools, parents can become intrusive. It is more likely that a teacher will enter a community where parents believe that the teachers mean to do well by their children and understand that the parents wish to function in a supportive partnership with the teachers.

Witnessing your own child progress through schools can quickly sensitize you to the many peculiar things that schools do to children, such as rejecting a homework assignment because the student's name is in the wrong place. On a very basic level, parents hope their children will be safe in school, and that includes preserving the health of a child's psyche. Parents hope that personnel in schools will respect the essential dignity of each child and will assume that parents are intelligent partners in learning. From this perspective, one can imagine the kind of practices that are likely to weaken relationships with parents: Don't return phone calls. Give students long, pointless homework assignments with ambiguous, incomplete, or unclear directions. Give students a steady diet of trivial classroom activities, like viewing irrelevant videos and doing daily "word searches." Publicly humiliate children by denigrating their intelligence or other personal characteristics. Be inflexible about deadlines and about making up missing schoolwork. Speak to parents in a condescending or patronizing way. Devise a convoluted and ponderous grading system that seems designed to baffle parents and penalize students. Offer untenable rationalizations for your mistakes, and never, ever admit fault.

On the flip side, teachers can do much to develop a strong bond with some parents or, at the very least, to avoid alienating them. Keep the lines of communication open with parents. Contacts can include letting parents know when their child is doing well, not just when the student gets in trouble. Provide assistance for the parents who are trying to figure out what is going on in the academic life of their child. It is best to assume that parents want to know whether a child has any homework and wish to assist in any way possible. Parents will especially want to know about long-term assignments and requirements for acquiring supplies and materials. Parents can be important partners if teachers communicate their expectations, convey an attitude of respect, share instructional plans, and solicit help with common concerns.

In summary, we have listed some basic guidelines for developing positive relationships with parents:

Developing Relationships with Parents

◆ Maintain a pattern of accessibility by phone, e-mail, or conferences.

◆ Place yourself in the position of the parent, who sees the personal impact you have on children.

◆ Recruit the parents to be partners with you in solving problems and advancing the education of their children.

◆ Practice active and attentive listening with parents, even when you think they are absolutely wrong, and especially when they are upset.

◆ Acknowledge fault when you've made mistakes, and suggest ways to correct errors.

◆ As frequently as possible, imagine that you are the parent trying to encourage and help your child do homework: it would be helpful to have clear, detailed instructions about what the child is supposed to do.

◆ Assume that somebody, somewhere, will read what you give your students in handouts, and the reader will closely scrutinize the material.

Relationships with Colleagues

When a person becomes a teacher, he or she enters a professional workplace, which will have its unique culture and its own expectations for professional conduct. For much of the school day, most teachers will work in isolation from other teachers. To make the world of work as rich, satisfying, and fun as possible, it makes good sense to avoid isolation and make connections with the rest of the staff. Work in an individual classroom will bear greater significance if the teacher is able to connect it with the work of others and recognize that his or her individual labors are connected to a community effort.

The first caution we offer, however, is the good advice our parents gave us during adolescence: stay away from the wrong crowd. It won't take long to figure out who the "wrong crowd" consists of. These individuals spend an inordinate amount of time in the teachers' lounge belittling students, griping about parents, sniping at the administration and school board, and generally complaining about every aspect of the school. An almost tangible cloud of cynicism and contempt hangs over them. At the same time, new teachers will be able to detect those staff members who like their students, respect the mission of schools, and remain positive and hopeful about the whole endeavor of teaching. These are the folks to seek out, befriend, and cling to.

Colleagues in schools have lives outside of school. Their interests, talents, beliefs, hopes, and fears combine to make them who they are. Just as they would do in developing a rapport with students, new teachers should seek to learn about their colleagues. Although not immediately apparent, there will be many connections and much common ground, and soon strong friendships will emerge. Initially it will be easiest to develop a bond with other new teachers. In some schools where several new teachers begin at the same time and experience induction together, new teachers develop a bond that parallels the experience of being members of the same graduating class: to a certain extent, they are sharing the same experience. As confidence grows, the circle of friends grows to include a variety of staff members who represent the diversity of the staff.

There will be occasions when new teachers join committees or otherwise work on projects with colleagues. As teachers leave teacher preparation programs, they can be left with the impression that they are now equipped with the latest, state-of-the-art methods and that the old-timers will labor with antiquated pedagogical practices. It would be safe to assume that experienced staff know much. It is also safe to assume that all adults like to have their knowledge and experience validated rather than dismissed. We caution, then, that new teachers proceed with an open mind. They do not necessarily have to embrace and use the ideas of others, but they can acknowledge gracefully their colleagues' contributions and withhold hasty judgment about the potential worth of these contributions.

Remember also that colleagues extend beyond the teaching staff. The various paraprofessionals and support staff play critical roles in the functioning of any school. Technicians, custodians, and clerical staff, among others, can make the difference between the smooth operation of a teacher's classroom and the crashing and burning of a teacher's plans. It is safe and decent to assume that everyone means to do a good job and deserves to be treated with dignity, respect, and gratitude. The following list summarizes some guidelines for developing the important collegial relationships at school:

Forming Relationships with Colleagues

◆ Find out who your colleagues are: their backgrounds, their talents, their expertise, their interests, their dreams, and their pet peeves.

◆ Gravitate toward those colleagues who convey a positive attitude and will not undermine your position by encouraging you to be destructively adversarial.

◆ Connect with colleagues through many informal meeting opportunities: having lunch, having coffee before school, taking a break, attending an activity or social function, or sharing rides.

◆ Graciously accept whatever instructional materials colleagues care to share with you, without feeling compelled to use them.

◆ Recognize the potential for using everyone for mentoring and support—from first-year teacher to forty-year veteran.

◆ Respect the dignity of every school employee, and recognize the generous and reliable support you receive from special staff members.

Relationships with Supervisors

It would be a dysfunctional school indeed that hired new teachers and looked for them to fail. The more likely situation is that school leaders hire those candidates whom they judge to have knowledge, skill, and potential. The supervisor's role, then, is to support professional development that will help newcomers realize their potential. The beginning teacher should begin a job with an understanding of and appreciation for this role. A positive working relationship will grow from a common understanding that the new teacher can rely on the supervisor to support his or her professional growth.

Even though it may seem like disclosing weaknesses, new teachers should seek the advice and support of the supervisor. They should begin with a frank discussion about what they are teaching, both the subject and the particular classes, and then rely on the supervisor to reply to some essential questions: What principles have guided the design of the curriculum? What is really important to teach? In the department, what are the common approaches to the teaching of writing, reading, and the study of literature? New teachers will either discover the underlying principles for instruction, which will allow for some flexibility and creativity, or they will realize there is no common ground or guiding principles, which poses other challenges in making instructional choices and employment decisions.

New teachers should work with school leaders to find inservice and other professional development opportunities. Participation in ongoing professional development will serve the new teacher's growth and signal to supervisors that he or she is invested in growing as a teacher. Despite an individual's long-term goals in education, the first obligation is to become the best teacher that individual can become, and that desire should be apparent to the supervisor.

Teachers should take advantage of the supervisor's obligation to help plan and solve problems. To that end, new teachers should discuss instructional plans, including projected lessons, frequently with the supervisor and rely on the supervisor to help them anticipate problems and explore alternatives to the original plans.

Supervisors are equipped to help in a variety of ways, but they will not be able to be of much assistance if new teachers do not communicate with them. If, for example, a beginning teacher is having difficulty managing a particular class, he or she can seek advice from a supervisor, and together they can devise a plan for making the situation better. If a teacher needs materials and resources to support lessons, a supervisor who knows about the need can help. If an angry parent means to dispute a grade or an instructional activity, the supervisor can be the most help if he or she knows the call is coming. The supervisor is the point person in inducting a new teacher into the world of teaching in a particular school and a particular department. The relationship is a key one; experienced teachers report that over time, as their confidence and trust has grown, the supervisor becomes another colleague, although a potentially important and influential one. We describe below a set of suggestions for building a relationship with a supervisor:

Building a Relationship with Your Supervisor

◆ Assume that your supervisor is primarily interested in your professional growth.

◆ Show through your professional activities that you are invested in your long-term professional development.

◆ Share with your supervisor your professional and instructional goals, and solicit support.

◆ Ask your supervisor to identify instructional priorities for your department, school, and district.

◆ Ask your supervisor to describe to you the behaviors that she or he thinks are characteristic of a good teacher.

◆ Invite your supervisor to troubleshoot to help you adjust an instructional plan.

◆ Alert your supervisor about approaching difficulties with parents or students.

◆ Realize that the distinction between your supervisor and your other colleagues will likely blur over time.

Handling the Workload

Teaching demands a commitment to long hours. In a sense, a teacher is always immersed in the business of teaching: after the actual hours in the classroom, a teacher plans, prepares, collaborates, grades, and reports. The long hours and the unremitting fatigue can quickly take a toll, as we describe in Chapter 6. Although this is an issue that induction programs seldom address, beginning teachers need to pay attention to basic issues of wellness. We confess to lack health care credentials, but we urge beginning teachers to eat regular healthy meals, exercise, sleep sufficient hours, avoid excessive caffeine consumption, drink lots of water, and wash their hands almost compulsively. Fatigue leaves a person vulnerable to infection, and in a school one can expect exposure to many sources of infection.

We urge beginning teachers to reserve and guard vigilantly their time for recreation and avocations. The many elements of our life that amuse us—reading, concerts, films, plays, collecting, building, etc.—make us whole and inform our teaching. We cringe to think of a teacher whose reading and dominant thought involve only his or her students' compositions and the literature of the high school curriculum. New teachers, like their experienced colleagues, need not be wracked with guilt for enjoying recreational reading, taking a bike ride, or viewing an escapist film. In fact, if they don't reserve time for such releases, teachers only add to existing stress.

Beginners need to look at the cycle of the school year. We generalize about this pattern in Chapter 6. Late fall is particularly hard on beginners, and if they are feeling especially worn out, discouraged, and sick at the end of October or the beginning of November, the feelings should not be surprising: they are sharing the same experience with almost every beginning teacher. Perhaps this is the part of the year when a homecoming to the college campus or a getaway weekend is in order to revitalize for the stretch toward the end of the term.

Experienced colleagues can provide a great deal of help by sharing materials, offering guidance for assessments, and explaining procedures for completing responsibilities in an efficient way. Colleagues can also help new teachers anticipate the periods of the school year that will be especially busy, which should help them pace the activities and paper load in classes. Experienced teachers usually avoid having all of their classes turn in compositions and complete major projects on the same day, two days before grades must be submitted. A look at the calendar with an experienced colleague can provide new teachers with much insight into how to pace themselves.

Some of the beginning teachers we interviewed noted that in their initial zeal they promised to return students' graded compositions in a matter of days. We caution teachers to make realistic goals and only make promises they are able to keep. It is wise to overestimate the time it will take to return graded papers and tests, while not procrastinating endlessly.

Finally, the beginning teachers in this study noted that one means of coping they embraced was the realistic recognition that things become progressively better over time. Planning becomes easier, grading becomes more efficient, and decision making becomes less daunting. In summary, we offer the following guidelines:

Handling the Workload

- ◆ Recognize that while the workload is initially daunting and continues to be taxing, it also gets better over time.

- ◆ Stagger tests, papers, and other major assignments or projects so that you are not deluged with paperwork.

- ◆ Announce reasonable goals for returning papers to students.

- ◆ Expect that by mid-October you will be very, very tired, and reassure yourself that it is natural to be exhausted at this time of year, knowing that before too long you will experience holiday breaks.

- ◆ Schedule some time each week for yourself—for rest, recreation, socializing, or enrichment.

- ◆ Pace yourself like an athlete by looking at the calendar to recognize the patterns of the year that require bursts of energy, and allow for reserving exhaustive effort.

- ◆ Rely on the help of colleagues who will share materials and show you managerial systems and shortcuts.

Knowledge of Subject/Curriculum

The presumption of many programs that offer teachers a "fast track" toward certification is that the two essential components of good teaching are well-developed communication skills and deep content knowledge. While we see this formula as too simplistic, we agree that teachers are well served if they are good communicators with a great deal of knowledge about their subject. Having a wealth of knowledge about the field of study allows teachers to judge what is really worth knowing. Of course, this prompts the question, "What is knowledge, and what knowledge is worth knowing?" We are ill-equipped to take on the question in depth here, but we invite the reader to explore the detailed and compelling discussions in Hillocks's *Ways of Thinking, Ways of Teaching* (1999), Scholes's *The Rise and Fall of English* (1998), and Applebee's *Curriculum as Conversation* (1996).

A transmission model of instruction dominates teaching in general and the teaching of English specifically (Goodlad, 1984; Applebee, 1991; Nystrand, 1997). If one views the teaching of English as essentially the telling of the story of the literature of a particular land and the reciting of a set of rules for grammar and usage, then the inexperienced teacher is in the impossible and futile position of trying to be the infallible source of literary knowledge. Scholes (1998) reminds us, "What I mean, then, by becoming an English teacher, includes a sense of one's own limitations, an awareness of how deep the sea of English is and how shallow and frail one's boat" (p. 70). A perusal of the learning standards listed for any state and the standards described by NCTE in partnership with the International Reading Association (1996) reveals a wide range of instructional goals and responsibilities. The number of possibilities is staggering. Where should one begin?

Wiggins and McTigue (1998) encourage educators to establish instructional goals by setting priorities and identifying the "big ideas" inherent in the field of study. Teachers battle the inclination to cover a lot of instructional ground without delving deeply into the exploration of big ideas. We suggest there is power in working out for oneself the priorities in teaching English—the big ideas, the essential processes, the habits of mind—and pursuing those priorities relentlessly. In order to set priorities, it is crucial once again for the new teacher to maintain dialogues with peers, mentors, and supervisors so that the various perspectives can guide and enrich the establishment of priorities.

If the emphasis in the classroom becomes the teaching of procedures—for reading, for writing, for speaking, and for thinking—then the teacher moves away from the role of sagacious transmitter of knowledge and into the role of supportive facilitator of the discovery and construction of meaning. The shift in roles is potentially liberating if the teacher has a firm understanding of the key goals or outcomes. We have seen a new teacher weep with envy when he saw a teacher from another school equipped with a detailed curriculum guide. The teacher was distressed because in his school he had simply been given the titles of the books designated for his classes and shown where his classroom was located. But while the detailed curriculum guide might seem very helpful, it can also be crippling if the teacher still has to follow someone else's plan, with no room for variation. These are two extremes—almost no guidance at all and guidance in overwhelming detail. An obvious alternative would involve an established curriculum guide that serves as a model, accompanied by conversations with a mentor and supervisor about how the curriculum was developed. The conversations would explore the underlying principles for the development of the curriculum, the significant outcomes, and the most powerful means for attaining the outcomes.

Our bias obviously is on the teaching of procedural knowledge: that is, knowing how to read and interpret, knowing how to write clearly and analytically, knowing how to express oneself in a rational and civil way, and knowing how to think critically. Consider this contrast: In planning a unit of instruction to study *Macbeth* with a group of twelfth graders, a new teacher might obsess about having a command of Scottish history, the life of Shakespeare, the history of the Elizabethan theater, the building specifications of the Globe Theatre, and other related information. An experienced teacher is likely to focus students' attention on how to work with the language of Shakespeare and how to interpret and evaluate the ideas of the play. One could argue that the interpretation of the play requires knowledge of Scottish history and the life of Shakespeare, but then the knowing would not be in isolation but would instead connect with and inform the reading of the play. Our advice to new teachers, then, is that if they are going to obsess about preparation, they should focus the preparation on the knowledge that is most important for the task at hand.

In the long term, a teacher's knowledge base develops with experience and with a lifelong effort to continue professional growth through classes, workshops, reading, and participation in professional meetings. The process begins, not ends, when the graduate leaves the teacher preparation program. Having some breadth of knowledge allows the teacher to make choices and adapt instruction as the context requires. Having some breadth of knowledge also allows the teacher to reflect on and judge what knowledge is worthy of attention. Here, then, is a brief list of recommendations related to the development of knowledge about the subject and the curriculum:

Building Knowledge of Subject and Curriculum

◆ Realize that your job is not simply to impart information to others, which is a model of teaching that unreasonably expects the teacher to command a vast reservoir of "facts" and never err.

◆ Consider that an essential part of the job is to raise doubts about significant questions that will guide inquiry.

◆ Focus on the teaching of procedural knowledge, and teach repeatedly those key habits of mind that bear repeating.

◆ Learn about the key concepts of and the theoretical foundation for the curriculum, and work within the framework that you recognize.

◆ Realize that a command of the curriculum develops over time and with the experience of working with the curriculum.

Evaluation and Grading

Long ago, Paul Diederich (1974) made the case that English teachers grade too much, and often without reliable measures. He reports that among the teachers he studied, "Most teachers had required a paper every two weeks from their students, and if they were conscientious about it, it took forty hours a week to grade, correct, and comment on them" (p. 4). He concludes: "Fewer and better measures at longer intervals of time are enough to show students, their parents, and their teachers how they are doing" (p. 4). The temptation, and the danger, for beginning teachers is to assign students to produce a lot of work and to attach a grade to everything: quizzes, homework, journals, tests, essays, and other products. The mere bulk of grades entered into the grade book might appear to have inherent reliability because the numbers are so grand; but the numbers are meaningless unless each assessment that adds to the aggregate is well constructed enough to allow the teacher to make a meaningful inference about a student's development.

Popham (2003) observes that "[a] test is only a representation, meaning that teachers must aim their instruction not at the tests, but toward the skill, knowledge, or affect that those tests represent" (p. 27). Popham reminds us that the assessment is a means for a teacher to make an inference about a student's understanding or mastery. And the inference is often a rough one, because few practitioners actually have the time or the wherewithal to develop carefully constructed assessments. Of course, some assessments can be sloppier than others. We encourage beginners to refer to the many useful resources (e.g., Diederich, 1974; Cooper & Odell, 1977; Stanford, 1979; Elbow, 1986, 1993; Yancey, 1992; Huot, 2002; Broad, 2003; Popham, 2003) for help in thinking about the broad issues of assessment and for practical advice for the assessment of writing and reading.

For new teachers, grading students' compositions will likely be the most time-consuming task they perform outside of the school day. Perhaps it seems intuitively reasonable to attempt to mark every error on every paper and write lengthy comments to help students improve their writing. But Hillocks (1982) reminds us, and experience tells us, that students are typically overwhelmed by detailed commentary and by the painstaking marking of errors. When the paper is covered with the teacher's editing marks and elaborate commentary, the writer finds it difficult to distinguish the relative gravity of the mundane typographical error from the more global and essential problems of organization, coherence, and logic. We advise, first of all, that the new teacher make a distinction between the kinds of commentary that different stages of the writing process require. In some stages, it makes good sense to rely on peer readers to provide commentary to the writers. Peer readers can perform some of the functions the teacher might otherwise assume as the only reader and editor of the papers. The teacher must also determine priorities for the current writing: What is the purpose for the writing? What features of writing did the teacher promote through instruction? What is really important in the current writing for this group of students at this stage in their development as writers? In setting priorities, the teacher establishes performance criteria for the assignment, rather than unreasonable perfection criteria.

We also encourage new teachers to consider the important instructional function of timely formative assessments that reveal to the teacher how instruction has affected learning. In a sense, the assessment of students' proficiencies becomes an assessment of the teacher's effectiveness. The data generated from formative assessments can prompt reflection and guide the teacher in making adjustments to the instructional plan. We suggest, in general, the following guidelines:

Grading and Evaluating

- Realize that it is unnecessary, and probably useless, to try to grade everything students do.

- Limit your assessments to a few carefully constructed, reasonably valid instruments.

- Make your assessment criteria explicit and fairly limited.

- Define evaluation criteria in a way that allows you to explain them to all students and defend them to parents.

- Check that your assessments are obviously connected to your instructional goals.

- Confer with your supervisor and your colleagues to be able to say with certainty what students should know and what they should be able to do as a result of your instruction.

Autonomy/Control

The beginning teachers in this study did not report feeling a great deal of pressure to follow a rigid curriculum, nor did they report that high-stakes tests and the No Child Left Behind legislation posed particular constraints on their freedom to choose what to teach and how to teach. At the same time, they expressed a vague worry that they might not be able to stay true to the pedagogical principles their university teacher education program promoted. In brief, they worried that the established curriculum or the common practices within a department would dictate what they would teach and how they would teach. Their concerns are reasonable, given the increased pressures on teachers of English to focus instruction on preparing students for the tests that will define to the public the quality of the school. Hillocks (2002) documents the very real dangers that broad-based tests pose to teacher autonomy and to the quality of English language arts instruction in the schools.

A good starting point in protecting autonomy is to take stock of what is important to teach for a particular group of students at a particular grade. Part of the thinking process would include a review of the state learning standards for English language arts and the standards expressed by the National Council of Teachers of English and the International Reading Association (1996). In a broader sense, teachers need to consider what are the compelling concepts and critical thinking processes and skills for a specific group of students. Teachers of English are likely to be thinking about these questions often; but for beginning teachers, it is especially important to write down the rationale for the content and approach for teaching a unit or course. A strong rationale will identify key concepts or "big ideas," explore their many facets and complexities, explain why these concepts are compelling and important for the learners, describe the integration of skills and critical thinking procedures, and defend the approach for the delivery of instruction. Smagorinsky (2002) offers a clear and detailed guide for producing rationales and has posted examples online (Smagorinsky, 2004) of the rationales that beginning teachers have written for a variety of units of instruction.

In conversations with supervisors, new teachers should share their rationales but should also remain open to questions and challenges. It is safe to assume that some thoughtful colleagues constructed an existing curriculum, and new teachers should not dismiss it entirely. The process of establishing what to teach and how to teach it involves dialogue and negotiation.

In some schools, attention to state learning standards is a

particular concern. New teachers will find, however, that if they remain true to the central goals for teaching the English language arts, they will be addressing many of the learning standards. In the same way that an actor will plan and perform by keeping in mind the "spine" of a play or a scene, a teacher will remain true to the guiding principles of a curriculum and a central mission for teaching.

Although beginning teachers might be concerned about the imposition of responsibilities and constraints on their creativity, in reality each teacher has a great deal of autonomy. Even in schools that have rigorous systems for teacher evaluation and professional development, the bulk of the teacher's time will be spent operating independently in the classroom. Most teachers have a lot of freedom in the classroom. The challenge is not so much to find ways to expand that freedom, but to learn what to do with it. The possible collision between the practices and values promoted in a methods class and the practices in a particular school and department is a situation that allows for the synthesis of ideas, or for the discovery that a particular setting is not a good match for the teacher and that it is time to find a better match. We offer, then, a brief list of related suggestions:

Protecting Autonomy

◆ Be aware of learning standards.

◆ Write rationales for what you teach and the way you teach it so that a specific approach is clear in your mind and you can support the approach in conversations with others.

◆ Discover the "spine" or overarching principles of the curriculum so that you can operate comfortably and creatively while remaining true to the basic principles.

◆ Be prepared to reassess what feels right, or what your university instructors seemed to advocate, as you try to reconcile your biases with the common practices in your school.

◆ Realize that seldom does anyone closely scrutinize what you do in your own classroom, and teachers must rely on their own conception of standards to judge responsibilities and to reflect on performance from day to day.

Physical and Personal Characteristics

The cases of Winnie and Christy, discussed in Chapter 3, illustrate some of the difficulties that beginning teachers might experience when they find that the students with whom they are working are quite different from the majority of the population where the teachers previously lived. The problem is not that the new teachers are the wrong shape, size, gender, color, or ethnicity; the problem seems to be that the new teachers are underprepared to negotiate the differences they are experiencing in a new environment. Obviously, teachers cannot change who they are, nor do we recommend that anyone make the attempt to change. The task, then, is to grow in knowledge of and appreciation for the differences that almost inevitably will exist.

During preservice training, prospective teachers need to visit many schools, especially those in the areas where the new teachers hope to work. Recognize the diversity in the schools, and learn about the interests and values that define populations in the schools and in the community. It is increasingly common for teacher education programs to build in a requirement to study multiculturalism as part of teacher training. This kind of academic background can help an observer appreciate the variety of cultures represented in a school.

The conversations a new teacher has with colleagues, supervisors, students, and their families will allow him or her to probe into the lives of the community in order to displace stereotypes and to learn about the values and significant issues that affect learners. Differences often frighten people because the differences represent an unknown; knowledge helps to combat stereotypes and reassures the newcomer.

Sometimes it is appropriate for a beginning teacher to make personal adjustments to adapt to a new environment. If, for example, the newly minted teacher has recently left college where he or she has spent most days in blue jeans and a sweatshirt, some adjustment in apparel might be in order to avoid being mistaken for a student. While some aspects of appearance seem superficial, and some rigidity in dress and demeanor can distance the teacher from students, teachers can play it safe by fashioning themselves as earnest professionals. Here are a few suggestions that might help ease the transition into a new environment:

Adjusting to Differences

- ◆ During teacher preparation, visit a variety of schools, especially schools in the area where you plan to work.

- ◆ Study multiculturalism by developing an appreciation of the literature, music, art, dance, food, and language that distinguish many cultures.

- ◆ Talk to staff members, students, and community members about the culture of the school and community and about the issues that are important to the community.

- ◆ Learn as much as possible about students in order to displace stereotypes and myths and to develop an honest appreciation for who the students really are.

- ◆ Gauge the culture of the school, and make adjustments to live up to the prevailing standards for professional appearance and decorum.

The lists of suggestions in this chapter are too long for anyone to keep in mind all at one time. We recommend two steps in using the lists. First, new teachers should consider the lists in a chronological way. Some steps should be taken before student teaching, some during student teaching, and some as they begin work as certificated teachers. As they consider the stage they are at in the training and induction process, they can focus on the needs of the moment and plan further for the next steps. New teachers should also be aware of priorities. We have indicated along the way what we judge to be the critical first steps in professional development. Furthermore, our summary in the next chapter limits the recommendations by setting some priorities.

Summary of Recommendations

The previous two chapters describe some measures that teacher education programs, high schools, and beginning teachers themselves can take to improve the experience of beginning a career in teaching English so that new teachers are more likely to remain to become skillful, experienced teachers. The recommendations derive from the expressed concerns of new teachers, from their reported means for coping, and from the actual practices of experienced teachers.

We have offered extensive, though not exhaustive, suggestions. We recognize that it is difficult to keep long lists of suggestions in mind, and it would be advantageous for new teachers, their university or school supervisors, and their mentors to focus on those actions that seem to be the top priorities. As we have formulated our recommendations, we have returned repeatedly to two factors that seem to cut across the many expressed concerns: (1) frustrations derive from the significant mismatch between expectations for teaching and the actual experience of teaching; and (2) new teachers struggle especially to shape a teacher persona. Keeping these two general concerns in mind, we offer a summary of five broad recommendations for teacher educators, school personnel, and new teachers themselves.

1. Working as partners, universities and schools should help prospective teachers to experience the realities of teaching through extensive clinical experiences, case study analyses, and visits from practicing teachers. To know what to expect from teaching, prospective teachers need to be in schools often. They need to do more than sit back and watch. They also need to enter into the life of the school and into the minds of teachers. When prospective teachers cannot go to schools, the schools can come to them by way of visits from experienced teachers and through the use of case studies to reveal the complexities of teaching and the potential challenges.

While visiting in schools, prospective teachers need to become involved in the experience of teaching by planning and teaching some lessons and by assessing the related outcomes. Visits to schools need to include interactions with students and conversations with teachers, all helping the newcomers anticipate what students are like and how teachers work and think.

Visits from experienced teachers to methods classes should move beyond discussions of the woes of managing unruly students and toward revealing the thinking processes of practicing teachers: why they teach, how they plan, and how they make decisions in and out of the classroom. When prospective teachers cannot experience the reality of schools firsthand, case studies can simulate some of the challenges they are likely to encounter so that the beginners can anticipate and develop the problem-solving strategies that experienced teachers form over time.

2. Teacher training programs should support prospective teachers in developing a teacher persona, a "public self," by allowing them to experience numerous occasions to assume the role of teacher: among peers, in schools, in various community settings. Whenever possible, prospective teachers need to experience the role of teacher. Some teacher education programs schedule a collaborative workshop to precede student teaching. In a workshop format, a team of preservice teachers plan a short unit of instruction, take turns teaching selected lessons, observe one another teach, and engage in reflective conversations about each lesson. The workshop process allows someone new to teaching to work in a supportive and relatively protected environment while figuring out some of the critical components of teaching, but especially while sorting out the image of a public self. If an individual begins student teaching, when the prospective teacher is usually operating independently, with a comfortable sense of who he or she is "supposed to" be, then the new teacher will have a great advantage over someone who is still sorting this out.

Familiarity with anything usually allows confidence to grow. Experienced teachers interviewed for this study reported feeling very comfortable with who they are, although it may have taken years to reach this point. The variety of experiences, the count-less interactions with students, through thousands of lesson epi-sodes, have allowed the experienced teachers to anticipate and choose, and have shaped them into confident professionals. Teacher education programs cannot compress and deliver those years of experience to a beginner, but the prospective teacher should never pass up an opportunity to assume the role of teacher and to pay attention to observers who might describe how the role fits.

3. In schools, beginning teachers should focus especially on build-ing positive relationships with students, without preoccupation about imposing order. Again, it may seem counterintuitive, but experienced teachers have reported to us that they are not preoc-cupied with establishing and maintaining order in the classroom by laying out a system of rules and consequences for breaking the rules. In the form of advice, this is what experienced teachers describe as their practice: convey your enthusiasm about the im-portance of, and interest in, the subject; acknowledge your ap-preciation of the fact that some students might be apprehensive; assure students of your expectation that they will be able to suc-ceed in the class; and announce a willingness to help outside of class time. While this is a general pattern of the way experienced teachers proceed with their classes, arriving at the point where the pattern is natural and comfortable will take some practice. It might even be worthwhile for new teachers to rehearse the open-ing day presentation in order to refine the message and the tone.

It takes time to develop a strong rapport with students. An obvious help in developing rapport is learning as much as pos-sible about the students. Knowledge about the academic and per-sonal background of each student will provide a means for connecting with their lives. Students long recall and greatly ap-preciate it when teachers attend the students' games, concerts, and performances and otherwise recognize their activities out-side the classroom.

Even though adolescence may not seem too distant from the current life of a new teacher, he or she would be well advised to learn about the general characteristics of adolescents. Current brain research reveals that the adolescent brain experiences significant changes during high school. A teacher will benefit from knowing that adolescents sometimes act in irrational ways and that for them, irrational is normal. The more teachers know about emerging adults, the less they will be shocked and disappointed when students don't act like mature grown-ups. Among groups of adolescents who are often rash, exuberant, and irrational, the key attributes for teachers are patience, tolerance, and understanding.

4. Supervisors, mentors, and other colleagues in schools should help new teachers anticipate and ease debilitating fatigue. In Chapter 6, we report that a common complaint among beginning teachers is that they are exhausted almost all the time. Typically, by the end of October or the beginning of November, new teachers have used up the lesson plans they developed before school began, have a mountain of papers to grade, and have been exposed to a potent host of viruses and bacteria. The impact of the fatigue is especially profound when the beginner is shocked by this new feeling of exhaustion.

We discuss in an earlier chapter some of the steps new teachers themselves can take to ease the fatigue and protect their health, but other people can help as well. Experienced colleagues, mentors, and supervisors can be proactive in helping the beginners anticipate the fatigue and find some relief. Pacing assignments, making reasonable promises, and being realistic about the preparation and performances that are possible are all practices that experienced teachers can reveal to their new colleagues. Experienced teachers must also be willing to share: lessons, tests, resources, strategies, and efficient procedures. And it is important to share early in the school year.

5. Trainers at the universities, and mentors and supervisors in schools, should encourage beginners to imitate the practices of skilled experienced teachers, even when those practices contradict the advice offered in new teacher "survival guides." Our review of popular guides for beginning teachers suggests to us that their advice, while well intentioned and sometimes insightful, is based more on the authors' generalizations from their own personal experiences rather than based on the trends among accomplished experienced teachers. We recommend in general that new teachers look to the practices of good experienced teachers for guidance in developing effective practices. Mentors and supervisors should also look to the actual practices of experienced teachers as guidelines and not rely solely on their recall of what they did as beginners. It requires some discipline to investigate whether one's intuitive sense of effective practices for new teachers is consistent with the practices actually reported by competent practitioners.

We cannot emphasize enough the importance of having positive, reliable mentors. We fear that the most vulnerable beginning teachers are those who enter the profession with many doubts about the students, their supervisors, and their own competence. When the newcomers team with cynical, pessimistic mentors, the combination is bound to confirm doubts and erode confidence. In contrast, if new teachers can look to the example of intelligent, positive, and supportive colleagues, in and out of school, they have brighter hope for the future and greater expectations for success.

Directions for Future Research

We have focused our attention on the concerns and coping strategies of beginning high school English teachers. These are the teachers with whom we have commonly worked, either in the university training for their teaching or in the supervision of their teaching in the schools. It would be valuable to rely on some of the same procedures to expand the research in order to look at a variety of teachers to see if the patterns vary among different contexts: by grade level, by subject, by school setting, and by the specific teacher training program.

While it would be valuable to replicate some phases of the research in a variety of settings to note distinctions, it would also be worthwhile to study the common findings between several studies of the concerns of beginning teachers. University instructors, supervisors, and beginning teachers would find it useful to know the common concerns and probable challenges that face all teachers, no matter the grade, teaching assignment, or school setting.

The survey of teacher expectations and experiences allowed us to contrast the anticipation of the preservice teachers with the actual experience of the practicing teachers. Further use of the survey will allow us to explore some of the nuances suggested by the current findings. A larger sample of survey data (more schools, from varied settings, and more participants) will be useful in completing analysis for these purposes: (1) identifying correlations between characteristics of setting and person and the concerns of the beginning teacher; and (2) clustering responses in order to profile categories of beginning teachers and their concerns. This research would be important in narrowing the focus of teacher preparation and mentor programs in order to differentiate between the needs of select groups of teachers. It would be worthwhile, for example, to know what Hispanic American women teaching in rural schools will be concerned about. As Nora, one of the participants in the study, reminds us, mentor programs that assume one size fits all can actually influence novices to leave teaching. Likewise, teacher preparation programs that offer a uniform, rigid model for teaching will not serve the needs of all participants.

In a limited way, we were able to follow beginning teachers for two or three years to track how their experiences changed over time. We see great promise in future research that involves longitudinal studies of teachers as they progress through an induction process over several years, from teacher preparation through the first five years of teaching, when many leave the profession. The research would help in mapping a long-term pattern of experience and would allow researchers to project the potentially critical periods as teachers move through their early career years.

We have suggested a number of actions that teacher training programs and schools might take to encourage teacher retention. Although we have drawn inferences from all the interviews and the survey data, we recognize that these are interpretations of the directions toward which the data point. Some interventions, like well-designed mentoring programs, have been supported and tested elsewhere. Many of our suggested interventions, however, have yet to be tested. We suggest that a series of studies to test the interventions will be needed to demonstrate their efficacy in influencing new teachers to remain in schools as teachers of English.

We see promise in the use of a set of problem-based scenarios that prompt beginners and experienced teachers to describe how they would address challenges common to teaching. We have relied on descriptions of the actions that participants *reported* they would take. It would be useful to accompany these reports with actual observations to confirm the patterns of responses among beginners and experienced teachers. A benefit of using the scenarios is that they can reveal ways of thinking that may be less evident in the responses to interview questions.

In general, we encourage further research into the induction and retention of teachers. We find the attrition of great numbers of talented teachers distressful, especially because of the devastating loss to the profession of the potential of these teachers and to the students whose lives they would affect. As we progressed in this study, we found more and more to investigate, and we had to devise a variety of means for answering the questions we raised; yet we believe we have just scratched the surface of the concerns, frustrations, and supports for beginning teachers. We hope the work continues and broadens our understanding of the factors that drive teachers away from schools, and the elements that are likely to keep the teachers in the classroom.

Appendix A

Novice Teachers: Interview Questions

1. Please indicate whether you are a <u>teacher</u> or a <u>student teacher</u>.

2. How long have you taught?

3. Describe a time during your student teaching or first year of teaching when you faced a troubling episode or aspect of the job. This would be something that occupied a lot of your thinking at the time and caused you considerable anxiety.

4. How did this challenging situation affect you? Could you recognize any physical and/or emotional effects that this challenge had on you?

5. How did you contend with the difficult situation? In other words, what steps did you take or strategies did you employ in order to endure the difficulty?

6. When you faced a difficult situation, what help was available to you? If you took advantage of the available help, what was the result? If you didn't seek any help, why didn't you?

7. What preparation during your teacher training, or assistance while you were teaching, could have helped you to make a difficult situation less stressful?

APPENDIX B

Teacher Expectation Survey

The purpose of this survey is to help researchers identify the expectations that preservice teachers have about their teaching <u>before</u> they begin their first teaching assignment. Your responses will remain anonymous and will be compiled with the responses of many other preservice teachers to reveal general trends in the expectations of those students who are preparing to become teachers. It should take you 10 to 15 minutes to complete the survey. Please mark all your responses on the answer sheet that you have been provided. <u>On the answer sheet, in the area provided for subject, please print the name of the college or university you now attend for teacher training.</u>

For each of the following items, judge the accuracy of the statement as you <u>anticipate</u> your teaching situation as you begin your teaching career. As you respond, try to imagine a likely teaching situation you will have in your first year of teaching. If you do not know exactly what your future teaching situation will be, <u>you necessarily will have to speculate in responding to the items.</u> For items 6 through 71, please respond by using the following scale:

a	=	not at all accurate
b	=	slightly accurate
c	=	somewhat accurate
d	=	mostly accurate
e	=	completely accurate

  1. Indicate whether you are male or female:

     a = male   b = female

  2. Please indicate your race/ethnicity:

     a = white   b = non-white

  3. Please indicate your age:

     a. = 19 to 22

    b. = 23 to 25

    c. = 26 to 30

    d. = 31 to 40

    e. = over 40

4. Characterize the type of school where you picture yourself working:

    a. = small public

    b. = large public

    c. = small private or parochial

    d. = large private or parochial

    e. = anywhere I can get a job

5. Please indicate the statement that best describes your current level of experience as part of your teacher preparation program:

    a. = no methods courses and no formal classroom observations or teaching experience

    b. = one or more methods courses but no formal classroom observations or teaching experience

    c. = one or more methods courses and formal classroom observations, but no teaching experience

    d. = presently student teaching

    e. = other

6. I will be free to choose my own instructional materials and methods.

7. I will enjoy a positive relationship with my professional colleagues.

8. My colleagues will respect my work.

9. My supervisors will know that they can rely on me to make sound educational choices.

10. My supervisors will see that I know my subject.

11. In my own classroom, I will work without the interference of others.

12. My ethnicity or skin color will not pose any conflicts in my teaching assignment.

13. My physical appearance will not cause me any problems in my role as teacher.

14. My gender will not be the source of conflicts in my work as a teacher.

15. I have been sufficiently trained for my first teaching assignment.

16. My students will know that I am in charge in my own classroom.

17. My students will know that I have expertise in my subject.

18. I will have a strong positive rapport with my students.

19. The parents of my students will respect me.

20. Students will recognize that I am fair in my grading and evaluation of their work.

21. My colleagues will recognize the knowledge and expertise that I bring to the job of teaching.

22. Students will appreciate my personality and my helping attitude.

23. My supervisors will be understanding and supportive.

24. The parents of my students will appreciate the efforts I am making to serve and support their children.

25. The parents of my students will recognize that I have their children's welfare in mind.

26. I will effectively and efficiently manage the paperwork that teaching requires.

27. Students in my classes will attend respectfully to my directions and reasonable requests.

28. My teaching colleagues will recognize that I work hard and am dedicated to my teaching.

29. My students will consistently complete their homework and their in-class assignments.

30. I will skillfully manage the time that the school requires for me to serve on committees, to supervise students, and to complete teaching responsibilities.

31. The planning of my lessons will not interfere with my spending time with family and friends.

32. Reading and grading my students' papers will not interfere with my doing the things that I love to do.

33. The workload involved in teaching is unlikely to have a deleterious effect on my physical health.

34. The demands of teaching will not have a negative impact on my emotional well-being.

35. I will quickly and easily master the curriculum that I am expected to teach.

36. Students will probably like and admire me.

37. I am confident that I can handle almost any teaching assignment that I am given in my subject.

38. I believe that I am sufficiently prepared to teach any course within my subject area in the school.

39. It will not be difficult for me to determine grades for my students.

40. Although time-consuming, the grading of my students' papers will be rather straightforward and relatively easy.

41. Students will recognize my authority as the subject matter expert in my classes.

42. Students will recognize my authority as the manager and leader of my classes.

43. My teacher training at the college or university will adequately serve me in my first teaching assignment.

44. My teacher training at the college or university has made me feel confident about my teaching.

45. It is unlikely that I will experience conflicts that are related to my gender.

46. It is unlikely that I will experience conflicts or challenges that are related to my physical appearance or physical stature.

47. It is unlikely that I will experience conflicts or challenges that are related to my skin color or to my ethnicity.

48. My skin color or ethnicity will not be an issue for my students.

49. I will be able to manage the requirements imposed on me by the school board and/or school administration.

50. I will operate autonomously, with little interference from school administrators.

51. My supervisors will recognize that I have provided students with appropriate and meaningful instruction.

52. My supervisors will see that I have command of the knowledge of my subject.

53. My supervisors will recognize that I make intelligent instructional decisions.

54. My colleagues will appreciate my work, and they will solicit my ideas.

55. My colleagues will be supportive and will eagerly share materials and ideas.

56. My personal and professional interactions with my colleagues will be pleasant and productive.

57. I will feel comfortable and confident about approaching my colleagues about school questions and about professional matters.

58. Experienced colleagues will serve as mentors to provide emotional and professional support.

59. My school will not limit me to following a prescribed curriculum.

60. My school will not pressure me to focus my instruction on preparing my students for local and state mandated tests.

61. I will be able to contribute to decisions that affect the school's English curriculum as a whole.

62. My teaching workload will not negatively affect my physical health.

63. My teaching experience will not negatively affect my emotional health.

64. I will manage my teaching responsibilities in a way that will allow me time for friends and family.

65. I will have sufficient time for preparation, committee work, and the supervision of students.

66. My colleagues at school will know that I work hard at my job.

67. Parents will know that I have their children's best interests at heart.

68. My supervisors will understand and support me.

69. Parents will show their respect for me.

70. Generally, students will like me.

71. Assessments of my students' performances will be fairly easy.

APPENDIX C

Teacher Experience Survey

The purpose of this survey is to help researchers identify the experiences that teachers have with their teaching <u>after</u> they have taught for some time. Your responses will remain anonymous and will be compiled with the responses of many other teachers to reveal general trends in the experiences of practicing teachers. It should take you 10 to 15 minutes to complete the survey. Please mark all your responses on the answer sheet that you have been provided. <u>On the answer sheet, in the area provided for subject, please print the name of the college or university that you judge to be primarily responsible for your teacher training.</u> When you have completed the survey, please place the survey and the answer sheet in the accompanying envelope, seal the envelope, and return the envelope to your department chair or other designated person at your school.

For each of the following items, judge the extent to which you agree or disagree with the statement about your current teaching situation. For items 6 through 71, please respond by using the following scale:

  a = not at all accurate
  b = slightly accurate
  c = somewhat accurate
  d = mostly accurate
  e = completely accurate

1. Indicate whether you are male or female:

 a = male   b = female

2. Please indicate your race/ethnicity:

 a = white   b = non-white

3. Please indicate your age:

 a. = 19 to 22

 b. = 23 to 25

 c. = 26 to 30

d. = 31 to 40

e. = over 40

4. Characterize the type of school where you work:

    a. = small public

    b. = large public

    c. = small private or parochial

    d. = large private or parochial

    e. = other

5. Please indicate your years of teaching experience since beginning your first teaching assignment:

    a. = 1 to 5

    b. = 6 to 10

    c. = 11 to 15

    d. = 16 to 20

    e. = 21 or more

6. I am free to choose my own instructional materials and methods.

7. I enjoy a positive relationship with my professional colleagues.

8. My colleagues respect my work.

9. My supervisors know that they can rely on me to make sound educational choices.

10. My supervisors see that I know my subject.

11. In my own classroom, I work without the interference of others.

12. My ethnicity or skin color does not pose any conflicts in my teaching assignment.

13. My physical appearance does not cause me any problems in my role as teacher.

14. My gender is not the source of conflicts in my work as a teacher.

15. I have been sufficiently trained for my current teaching assignment.

16. My students know that I am in charge in my own classroom.

17. My students know that I have expertise in my subject.

18. I have a strong positive rapport with my students.

19. The parents of my students respect me.

20. Students recognize that I am fair in my grading and evaluation of their work.

21. My colleagues recognize the knowledge and expertise that I bring to the job of teaching.

22. Students appreciate my personality and my helping attitude.

23. My supervisors are understanding and supportive.

24. The parents of my students appreciate the efforts I am making to serve and support their children.

25. The parents of my students recognize that I have their children's welfare in mind.

26. I effectively and efficiently manage the paperwork that teaching requires.

27. Students in my classes attend respectfully to my directions and reasonable requests.

28. My teaching colleagues recognize that I work hard and am dedicated to my teaching.

29. My students consistently complete their homework and their in-class assignments.

30. I skillfully manage the time that the school requires for me to serve on committees, to supervise students, and to complete teaching responsibilities.

31. The planning of my lessons does not interfere with my spending time with family and friends.

32. Reading and grading my students' papers does not interfere with my doing the things that I love to do.

33. The workload involved in teaching does not have a deleterious effect on my physical health.

34. The demands of teaching do not have a negative impact on my emotional well-being.

35. I have quickly and easily mastered the curriculum that I am expected to teach.

36. Students like and admire me.

37. I am confident that I can handle almost any teaching assignment that I am given in my subject.

38. I believe that through my teacher training I was sufficiently prepared to teach any course within my subject area in the school.

39. It is not difficult for me to determine grades for my students.

40. Although time-consuming, the grading of my students' papers is rather straightforward and relatively easy.

41. Students recognize my authority as the subject matter expert in my classes.

42. Students recognize my authority as the manager and leader of my classes.

43. My teacher training at the college or university adequately served me in my first teaching assignment.

44. My teacher training at the college or university has made me feel confident about my teaching.

45. I have not experienced conflicts that are related to my gender.

46. I have not experienced conflicts or challenges that are related to my physical appearance or physical stature.

47. I have not experienced conflicts or challenges that are related to my skin color or to my ethnicity.

48. My skin color or ethnicity is not an issue for my students.

49. I am easily able to manage the requirements imposed on me by the school board and/or school administration.

50. I operate autonomously, with little interference from school administrators.

51. My supervisors recognize that I have provided students with appropriate and meaningful instruction.

52. My supervisors see that I have command of the knowledge of my subject.

53. My supervisors recognize that I make intelligent instructional decisions.

54. My colleagues appreciate my work, and they solicit my ideas.

55. My colleagues are supportive and eagerly share materials and ideas.

56. My personal and professional interactions with my colleagues are pleasant and productive.

57. I am comfortable and confident about approaching my colleagues about school questions and about professional matters.

58. Experienced colleagues have served as mentors to provide me with emotional and professional support.

59. My school does not limit me to following a prescribed curriculum.

60. My school does not pressure me to focus my instruction on preparing my students for local and state mandated tests.

61. I am able to contribute to decisions that affect the school's English curriculum as a whole.

62. My teaching workload does not negatively affect my physical health.

63. My teaching experience does not negatively affect my emotional health.

64. I manage my teaching responsibilities in a way that allows me time for friends and family.

65. I have sufficient time for preparation, committee work, and the supervision of students.

66. My colleagues at school know that I work hard at my job.

67. Parents know that I have their children's best interests at heart.

68. My supervisors understand and support me.

69. Parents show their respect for me.

70. Generally, students like me.

71. Assessments of my students' performances are fairly easy.

Appendix D

Novice Teachers
Follow-up Interview Questions and Protocol

If the subject is <u>no longer teaching</u>, ask these questions:

1a. Why are you no longer teaching?

1b. Do you plan to return to teaching some day? Why? Why not?

If the subject <u>continues to teach</u>, ask these questions:

1c. Why have you continued to teach?

1d. Do you plan to continue to teach in the future? Why? Why not?

If the subject <u>no longer teaches</u>, ask these questions:

2a. What could the school have done to encourage you to remain in teaching?

2b. What could your teacher education program have done to encourage you to remain in teaching?

If the subject <u>continues to teach</u>, ask these questions:

2c. What can the school do to encourage you to remain in teaching?

2d. What can teacher education programs do to encourage you (prepare teachers) to remain in teaching?

If the subject <u>no longer teaches</u>, ask this question:

3a. What would influence you, or prepare you, to return to teaching?

If the subject <u>continues to teach</u>, ask this question:

3b. What do you have to do personally to remain in teaching?

For <u>all subjects</u>, ask this question:

    4a. How has your life changed, if at all, since our first interview?

If the subject <u>continues to teach</u>, ask this question:

    4b. How has your experience as a teacher changed, if at all, since our first interview?

APPENDIX E

Questionnaire: Teacher Reflection

<u>Directions:</u> Your written responses to the following questions will help researchers to track the development of teachers during their first year of teaching. To complete this questionnaire, please follow this procedure:

1. Respond to each prompt <u>before</u> you discuss the scenarios or questions with anyone. It is very important that you complete your responses independently, without consulting any other person.

2. For each of the scenarios, write a description of how <u>you</u> would react to the situation.

3. If you need additional room to write your responses, please write them on the back of the paper.

4. Be prepared to talk to the researcher about the reactions that you have to the scenarios.

Thank you for your assistance.

Scenario 1

Two young women, Julia and Gracie, in the last period class have been at odds all school year. They sit two rows away from each other. In the current lesson, the class discusses the relative morality of a character in a story. Julia blurts out, "She's a whore, just like Gracie." The students all say "Ooooh!" Then one says, "You've been dissed, Gracie." Gracie seems to grit her teeth, ready to pounce. The room is tense.

Please explain what you would do in this situation:

_____
_____
_____
_____
_____
_____
_____
_____
_____
_____
_____

Scenario 2

At the end of the school day, the teacher finds a written phone message in the mailbox. The message is from a parent with whom the teacher had already had a tense conference about a student's low grades. Today, the teacher returned a test on which the same student had received a failing grade. The message asks the teacher to return the call <u>as soon as possible</u>.

Please explain what you would do in this situation:

_____
_____
_____
_____
_____
_____
_____
_____
_____
_____
_____

Scenario 3

The teacher arrives at his/her classroom ten minutes before 1st period class is to begin. The teacher opens his/her briefcase to discover that all the lesson materials are still at home on the kitchen table. The materials include the papers that the teacher had stayed up until 1:00 a.m. grading in order to fulfill a promise to return the papers today. The teacher does not have the transparency and the handouts that he/she was going to rely on to introduce a novel that the class would begin reading together.

Please explain what you would do in this situation:

_____
_____
_____
_____
_____
_____
_____
_____
_____

Scenario 4

On Friday afternoon, a teacher reflects on the next four days that lie ahead. The teacher has two tests and three sets of essays that have to be graded and a backlog of homework assignments that still must be posted in the grade book. The teacher must serve as judge and chaperone at a speech tournament at a distant school on Friday evening and all day Saturday. It is the end of the current grading period and grades are due at the principal's office by 8:00 a.m. on the following Wednesday. Monday is the start of the new grading period when the teacher hopes to begin a new literature unit.

Please explain what you would do in this situation:

_____
_____
_____
_____
_____
_____
_____
_____

Scenario 5

The teacher anticipates that in two weeks he/she will begin teaching Albert Camus' <u>The Fall</u> in a senior advanced placement class. This is the first time that the teacher has taught the class and he/she has just finished reading the novel for the first time. The students in the class are very bright, and they are astute readers. In class, they often ask questions that challenge the teacher's knowledge and expertise about the literature. The advanced placement curriculum that the experienced advanced placement teachers have constructed for the AP program specifies that the students study <u>The Fall</u> at this time.

Please explain what you would do in this situation:

_____
_____
_____
_____
_____
_____
_____

Scenario 6

In the staff lounge, a teacher hears a colleague describe how he selects what he judges to be some of the weaker compositions from his ninth-grade class, makes transparencies of the compositions, and projects them in class for critique. Although he obscures each student's name, the teacher criticizes the faults of the composition in great detail. The teacher who overhears the colleague also recalls passing the teacher's classroom and briefly observing him as he ridiculed a student's composition. Although no name appeared on the transparency, the writer would recognize the paper, and one had to wonder if other students might recognize who wrote the composition. It appeared to the observer that the students in class showed signs of being uncomfortable as they witnessed the harsh critique.

Please explain what you would do in this situation:

_____
_____
_____
_____
_____
_____
_____

Scenario 7

A teacher received a note from his supervisor that she would soon visit his seventh-period class for a formal observation that would be part of his evaluation for the year. In her note, the supervisor indicates that she must complete the observations soon and the specified date is the only time that fits into her busy schedule. The teacher recognizes that the date for the observation is the day that the teacher returns to school after being out of school to attend a two-day conference. The seventh period is when the teacher's low-ability sophomore class meets immediately after lunch.

Please explain what you would do in this situation:

_____
_____
_____
_____
_____
_____
_____

APPENDIX F

Questionnaire: Teacher Reflection

<u>Directions:</u> Your written responses to the following questions will help researchers to track the development of teachers during their years of teaching. To complete this questionnaire, please follow this procedure:

1. Respond to each prompt <u>before</u> you discuss the scenarios or questions with anyone. It is very important that you complete your responses independently, without consulting any other person.

2. First, take a few minutes to recall your experiences as a teacher during your <u>first year</u> of teaching.

3. For each of the scenarios, write a description of how <u>you</u> would have reacted to the situation during your <u>first year of teaching</u>. Then write a description of the way you would react to the situation now.

4. If you note <u>any differences</u> between the way you would have reacted during your first year of teaching and the way that you would react today, explain why you think there are those differences.

5. If you need additional room to write your responses, please write them on the back of the paper.

6. Be prepared to talk to the researcher about the reactions that you predict and about any differences that you perceive

Thank you for your assistance.

Scenario 1

Two young women, Julia and Gracie, in the last period class have been at odds all school year. They sit two rows away from each other. In the current lesson, the class discusses the relative morality of a character in a story. Julia blurts out, "She's a whore, just like Gracie." The students all say "Ooooh!" Then one says, "You've been dissed, Gracie." Gracie seems to grit her teeth, ready to pounce. The room is tense.

What would you have done in this situation when you <u>first</u> <u>started teaching</u>?

What would you do <u>now</u> in this situation?

_____

_____

_____

_____

_____

_____

_____

If you notice any differences between the two responses above, explain here why there would be these differences.

_____

_____

_____

_____

Scenario 2

At the end of the school day, the teacher finds a written phone message in the mailbox. The message is from a parent with whom the teacher had already had a tense conference about a student's low grades. Today, the teacher returned a test on which the same student had received a failing grade. The message asks the teacher to return the call <u>as soon as possible</u>.

What would you have done in this situation when you <u>first started teaching</u>?

_____

_____

_____

_____

_____

_____

_____

What would you do <u>now</u> in this situation?

_____

_____

_____

_____

_____

_____

_____

If you notice any differences between the two responses above, explain here why there would be these differences.

_____

_____

_____

_____

Scenario 3

The teacher arrives at his/her classroom ten minutes before 1st period class is to begin. The teacher opens his/her briefcase to discover that all the lesson materials are still at home on the kitchen table. The materials include the papers that the teacher had stayed up until 1:00 a.m. grading in order to fulfill a promise to return the papers today. The teacher does not have the transparency and the handouts that he/she was going to rely on to introduce a novel that the class would begin reading together.

What would you have done in this situation when you <u>first</u> <u>started teaching</u>?	What would you do <u>now</u> in this situation?
_____	_____
_____	_____
_____	_____
_____	_____
_____	_____
_____	_____
_____	_____

If you notice any differences between the two responses above, explain here why there would be these differences.

_____

_____

_____

_____

Scenario 4

On Friday afternoon, a teacher reflects on the next four days that lie ahead. The teacher has two tests and three sets of essays that have to be graded and a backlog of homework assignments that still must be posted in the grade book. The teacher must serve as judge and chaperone at a speech tournament at a distant school on Friday evening and all day Saturday. It is the end of the current grading period and grades are due at the principal's office by 8:00 a.m. on the following Wednesday. Monday is the start of the new grading period when the teacher hopes to begin a new literature unit.

What would you have done in this situation when you <u>first started teaching</u>?

What would you do <u>now</u> in this situation?

_____

_____

_____

_____

_____

_____

_____

_____

_____

_____

_____

_____

_____

_____

If you notice any differences between the two responses above, explain here why there would be these differences.

_____

_____

_____

_____

Scenario 5

The teacher anticipates that in two weeks he/she will begin teaching Albert Camus' The Fall in a senior advanced placement class. This is the first time that the teacher has taught the class and he/she has just finished reading the novel for the first time. The students in the class are very bright, and they are astute readers. In class, they often ask questions that challenge the teacher's knowledge and expertise about the literature. The advanced placement curriculum that the experienced advanced placement teachers have constructed for the AP program specifies that the students study The Fall at this time.

What would you have done in this situation when you first started teaching?

What would you do now in this situation?

_____ _____

_____ _____

_____ _____

_____ _____

_____ _____

_____ _____

If you notice any differences between the two responses above, explain here why there would be these differences.

_____

_____

_____

_____

Scenario 6

In the staff lounge, a teacher hears a colleague describe how he selects what he judges to be some of the weaker compositions from his ninth-grade class, makes transparencies of the compositions, and projects them in class for critique. Although he obscures each student's name, the teacher criticizes the faults of the composition in great detail. The teacher who overhears the colleague also recalls passing the teacher's classroom and briefly observing him as he ridiculed a student's composition. Although no name appeared on the transparency, the writer would recognize the paper, and one had to wonder if other students might recognize who wrote the composition. It appeared to the observer that the students in class showed signs of being uncomfortable as they witnessed the harsh critique.

What would you have done in this situation when you <u>first</u> <u>started teaching</u>?	What would you do <u>now</u> in this situation?
_____	_____
_____	_____
_____	_____
_____	_____
_____	_____
_____	_____
_____	_____

If you notice any differences between the two responses above, explain here why there would be these differences.

_____

_____

_____

_____

Scenario 7

A teacher received a note from his supervisor that she would soon visit his seventh-period class for a formal observation that would be part of his evaluation for the year. In her note, the supervisor indicates that she must complete the observations soon and the specified date is the only time that fits into her busy schedule. The teacher recognizes that the date for the observation is the day that the teacher returns to school after being out of school to attend a two-day conference. The seventh period is when the teacher's low-ability sophomore class meets immediately after lunch.

What would you have done in this situation when you <u>first</u> started teaching?

What would you do <u>now</u> in this situation?

_____

_____

_____

_____

_____

_____

_____

_____

_____

_____

_____

_____

_____

_____

If you notice any differences between the two responses above, explain here why there would be these differences.

_____

_____

_____

_____

APPENDIX G

Protocol for Case Studies of Three First-Year Teachers

During September
Initial interview: What classes are you teaching? What are your impressions of the school and the students? What has been the high point of your experience so far? What challenges do you face and what concerns do you have at this point? What support do you have in the school to help you face challenges? To what extent do you rely on help from outside the school? How well has your college or university program prepared you for you current teaching experience?

Late October
Interview and classroom observation: How have you been able to contend with the curriculum you have been assigned to teach? How much time do you typically spend each day, and on weekends, to prepare for lessons and to grade papers? How has the workload affected you? General impressions from the lesson observed: classroom management/rapport, knowledge, pedagogy.

December
Third interview: Are there changes from the original responses: What has been the high point of your experience so far? What challenges do you face and what concerns do you have at this point? What support do you have in the school to help you face challenges? To what extent do you rely on help from outside the school? How well has your college or university program prepared you for you current teaching experience?

Early March
Fourth interview: focus on supervision/teacher evaluation. Describe your rapport with your supervisor(s). Describe the teacher evaluation process. To what extent does the teacher evaluation program support your professional development? To what extent have your colleagues been helpful in supporting your development as a teacher? To what extent has your teaching experience changed during the course of the school

year: relationship with students, colleagues, supervisors, parents; handling workload, command of subject/curriculum, grading/assessment, autonomy?

Second observation: What changes do you perceive from the first to the second observation?

Late May

Fifth interview: As you reflect on your first year of teaching, what were the most memorable experiences? What were the greatest challenges? What advice would you offer to someone who was beginning his or her first year of teaching? What advice would you offer school administrators to guide their efforts toward supporting new teachers and encouraging their retention? What advice would you offer the directors of teacher training programs to prepare new teachers to enter and remain in the profession?

Case Studies: Each observer writes a case study to summarize the experience of the first-year teacher: setting, noteworthy responses to interview questions, reflections on the classroom observations, citations from the teacher's reflection on the whole school year.

Analysis: Each observer reads all three case studies and identifies patterns of experience. The observers discuss the trends and describe the common pattern for the first year of teaching.

May, Year Two

One researcher met with the subjects of the case studies at the end of their second year of teaching. The following questions guided the interviews: As you reflect on your first two years of teaching, what were the most memorable experiences? Why? What were the greatest challenges? Why? What advice would you offer to someone who was beginning his or her teaching career? What advice would you offer school administrators to guide their efforts toward supporting new teachers and encouraging their retention? What advice would you offer the directors of teacher training programs to prepare new teachers to enter and remain in the profession? How have things been different (or have they been?) from what you thought your first two years would be like? If you could change anything about your first two years, what would it be and why? What is the most important thing you have learned about teaching during your first two years? How have things changed for you, if at all, since our last interview last year?

Appendix H

Experienced Teachers' Interview Questions and Protocol

1a. Describe your experience in handling the workload (including paper grading) that you faced when you began teaching.

1b. To what extent has your experience in handling the workload changed since you began teaching?

2a. How would you characterize the relationship you had with your supervisor(s) when you began teaching?

2b. To what extent has your relationship with your supervisor(s) changed since you began teaching?

3a. How would you characterize your relationship with students (including your classroom management experience) when you began teaching?

3b. To what extent has your relationship with students changed during the course of your career in teaching?

4a. When you began teaching, to what extent did you believe you had license to teach the way you wanted to teach and had influence on the curriculum within your department?

4b. To what extent has your sense of autonomy and influence changed since you began teaching?

5a. Describe the extent to which you found grading and evaluation a challenge when you began teaching?

5b. To what extent has your experience with grading and evaluation changed since you began teaching?

6a. When you began teaching, how did your physical appearance and other personal characteristics affect your ability to do your job?

6b. To what extent have you experienced a change in the way that your physical appearance and other personal characteristics affect your ability to do your job?

Appendix I

Analysis of Interviews of Experienced Teachers

TO: Reader
FROM: Tom McCann, Larry Johannessen, Barney Ricca
DATE:
SUBJECT: Analysis of Interviews of Experienced Teachers

Thank you for your willingness to assist us in analyzing a set of transcripts of interviews with experienced teachers. The series of interviews with experienced teachers was intended to probe them to account for the change in their professional approaches and in their perceptions of themselves in regard to the following categories: handling the workload, relationship with supervisors, relationships with students, autonomy, grading/evaluation, and personal characteristics. For the purposes of the interviews, we defined the categories in this way:

- handling the workload: the physical, intellectual, and emotional demands of the job, including the work in the classroom, the preparation and grading in the evening and on weekends, extracurricular responsibilities, and other clerical and managerial duties;

- relationship with supervisors: the rapport with the supervisors, especially with the immediate supervisor, who would have the greatest influence on the evaluation of job performance;

- relationships with students: the rapport that the teacher experiences with students, which includes any issues and strategies related to classroom management;

- autonomy: the extent to which the teacher can make decisions about the content and procedures for instruction and the extent to which the organization imposes policies and content on the teacher;

- grading/evaluation: the issues related to making judgments about students' performances and reporting those judgments to students and parents;

◆ <u>personal characteristics</u>: the teacher's awareness and perhaps self-consciousness about personal characteristics such as gender, body shape and size, ethnicity, and age, and the extent to which these characteristics influence thinking and performance.

After you have read all the transcripts, please indicate, in regard to these six categories, what is the <u>pattern</u> of response to the following questions?

◆ In <u>what ways</u> have teachers changed from their first year of teaching to the current year, after they have taught for at least ten years?

◆ According to the experienced teachers, what has <u>influenced</u> or <u>caused</u> their change over the years?

Please write your observations in the form of a conceptual memo. We are looking for <u>overall patterns</u>, rather than distinctive comments from each teacher. The memo does not need to be lengthy (probably one to two pages), but it should provide some observations about each of the six categories.

APPENDIX J

Scenario Interview Questions and Protocol

For EACH scenario, ask the novice teacher if he/she has noticed any difference in the responses (i.e., novice vs. veteran). Depending on the response, follow sequence #1 or #2. After discussing all of the scenarios, follow sequence #3.

1a. If you notice any differences between the way a veteran teacher responded to the situation and the way that you responded, how would you explain the differences?

1b. If the veteran teacher took a different approach, do you agree with the actions that he/she took?

1c. If you disagree, explain why.

1d. If you agree with the veteran teacher's approach, but you have not taken the same approach, explain why the other teacher can be different yet correct or appropriate.

2. If you and the veteran teacher had essentially the same response to the situation, how do you explain that you would have the same insights and inclinations as a teacher with much more experience?

3a. In the end, why aren't you more like the veteran teacher?

3b. If the person says, "because he/she is older and more experienced," prompt the novice teacher to explain why this would make a difference.

3c. If the person says, "because he/she has a much different personality," prompt the novice teacher to explain why this would make a difference.

3d. If the person says, "because he/she is much smarter or more knowledgeable," prompt the novice teacher to explain why this would make a difference.

BIBLIOGRAPHY

Andrews, K. R. (Ed.). (1953). *The case method of teaching human relations and administration: An interim statement.* Cambridge: Harvard University Press.

Andrews, K. R. (1954). The role of the instructor in the case method. In M. P. McNair (Ed.), *The case method at the Harvard Business School: Papers by present and past members of the faculty and staff.* New York: McGraw-Hill.

Applebee, A. N. (1991). Environments for language teaching and learning: Contemporary issues and future directions. In J. Flood et al. (Eds.), *Handbook of research on teaching the English language arts* (pp. 549–56). New York: Macmillan.

Applebee, A. N. (1996). *Curriculum as conversation: Transforming traditions of teaching and learning.* Chicago: University of Chicago Press.

Ausubel, D. P. (2000). *The acquisition and retention of knowledge: A cognitive view.* Dordrect, Neth.: Kluwer.

Bloom, B. S. (1982). *Human characteristics and school learning.* New York: McGraw-Hill.

Boe, E. E., Bobbitt, S. A., Cook, L. H., Whitener, S. D., & Weber, A. L. (1996). *Predictors of retention, transfer, and attrition of special and general education teachers: Data from the 1989 Teacher Followup Survey.* Washington, DC: Office of Educational Research and Improvement, National Center for Education Statistics, U.S. Department of Education.

Borko, H., & Putnam, R. T. (1996). Learning to teach. In D. C. Berliner & R. C. Calfee (Eds.), *Handbook of educational psychology* (pp. 673–708). New York: Macmillan.

Broad, B. (2003). *What we really value: Beyond rubrics in teaching and assessing writing.* Logan: Utah State University Press.

Cooper, C. R., & Odell, L. (1977). *Evaluating writing: Describing, measuring, judging.* Urbana, IL: National Council of Teachers of English.

Costa, A. L., & Garmston, R. J. (2002). *Cognitive coaching: A foundation for renaissance schools* (2nd ed.). Norwood, MA: Christopher-Gordon.

Darling-Hammond, L. (1997). *Doing what matters most: Investing in quality teaching*. New York: National Commission on Teaching & America's Future.

Darling-Hammond, L. (2000). *Solving the dilemmas of teacher supply, demand, and standards: How we can ensure a competent, caring, and qualified teacher for every child*. New York: National Commission on Teaching and America's Future.

Darling-Hammond, L. (2003). Keeping good teachers: Why it matters, what leaders can do. *Educational Leadership, 60*(8), 6–13.

Darling-Hammond, L., & Youngs, P. (2002). Defining "highly qualified teachers": What does "Scientifically-based research" actually tell us? *Educational Researcher, 31*(9), 13–25.

De Voto, B. (Ed.). (1976). *The portable Mark Twain*. New York: Viking.

Diederich, P. B. (1974). *Measuring growth in English*. Urbana, IL: National Council of Teachers of English.

Educational Resources Information Center. (1998). *A back to school report on the baby boom echo: America's schools are overcrowded and wearing out*. Washington, DC: Office of Educational Research and Improvement, U.S. Department of Education.

Elbow, P. (1986). *Embracing contraries: Explorations in learning and teaching*. New York: Oxford University Press.

Elbow, P. (1993). Ranking, evaluating, and liking: Sorting out three forms of judgment. *College English, 55*(2), 187–206.

Erickson, F. (1986). Qualitative methods in research on teaching. In M. C. Wittrock (Ed.), *Handbook of research on teaching* (3rd ed., pp. 119–61). New York: Macmillan.

Featherstone, H. (1993). Learning from the first years of classroom teaching: The journey in, the journey out. *Teachers College Record, 95*(1), 93–112.

Feiman-Nemser, S. (2003). What new teachers need to learn. *Educational Leadership, 60*(8), 25–29.

Freeman, S. C., Dienstbier, R. A., Roesch, S. C., & Sime, W. (2000). Psychological preparation for anaesthesia and the facial EMG: Revealing physiological patterns. In C. Jordan, D. J. A. Vaughan, & D. E. F. Newton (Eds.), *Memory and awareness in anaesthesia IV* (pp. 248–61). London: Imperial College Press.

Fuller, F. F. (1969). Concerns of teachers: A developmental conceptualization. *American Educational Research Journal, 6*(2), 207–26.

Gerald, D. E., & Hussar, W. J. (1998). *Projections of education statistics to 2008* (27th ed.). Washington, DC: Office of Educational Research and Improvement, National Center for Educational Statistics, U.S. Department of Education. (NCES 98-016)

Goodlad, J. I. (1984). *A place called school: Prospects for the future.* New York: McGraw-Hill.

Grossman, P., Thompson, C., & Valencia, S. (2001). *District policy and beginning teachers: Where the twain shall meet.* Seattle: Center for the Study of Teaching and Policy, University of Washington.

Henke, R. R. et al. (1997). *America's teachers: Profile of a profession, 1993–94.* Washington, DC: Office of Educational Research and Improvement, National Center for Education Statistics, U.S. Department of Education.

Henke, R. R., Chen, X., & Geis, S. (2000). *Progress through the teacher pipeline: 1992–93 college graduates and elementary/secondary teaching as of 1997.* Washington, DC: Office of Educational Research and Improvement, National Center for Educational Statistics, U.S. Department of Education.

Hillocks, G., Jr. (1982). The interaction of instruction, teacher comment, and revision in teaching the composing process. *Research in the Teaching of English, 16,* 261–78.

Hillocks, G., Jr. (1999). *Ways of thinking, ways of teaching.* New York: Teachers College Press.

Hillocks, G., Jr. (2002). *The testing trap: How state writing assessments control learning.* New York: Teachers College Press.

Huot, B. (2002). *(Re)articulating writing assessment for teaching and learning.* Logan: Utah State University Press.

Hussar, W. J. (1999a). Predicting the need for newly hired teachers in the United States to 2008–09. *Education Statistics Quarterly, 1*(4), 45–50.

Hussar, W. J. (1999b). *Predicting the need for newly hired teachers in the United States to 2008–09.* Washington, DC: Office of Educational

Research and Improvement, National Center for Education Statistics, U.S. Department of Education. (NCES 1999-026)

Ingersoll, R. M. (2001). *Teacher turnover, teacher shortages, and the organization of schools.* Seattle: Center for the Study of Teaching and Policy, University of Washington.

Ingersoll, R. M. (2002). The teacher shortage: A case of wrong diagnosis and wrong prescription. *NASSP Bulletin, 86*(631), 16–31.

Ingersoll, R. M., & Smith, T. M. (2003). The wrong solution to the teacher shortage. *Educational Leadership, 60*(8), 30–33.

Johannessen, L. R., & McCann, T. M. (2002). *In case you teach English: An interactive casebook for prospective and practicing teachers.* Upper Saddle River, NJ: Merrill/Prentice Hall.

Johnson, S. M. (2004). *Finders and keepers: Helping new teachers survive and thrive in our schools.* San Francisco: Jossey-Bass.

Kellough, R. D. (1999). *Surviving your first year of teaching: Guidelines for success.* Upper Saddle River, NJ: Merrill.

Kottler, E., Kottler, J. A., & Kottler, C. J. (1998). *Secrets for secondary school teachers: How to succeed in your first year.* Thousand Oaks, CA: Corwin Press.

Leserman, J., Stuart, E. M., Mamish, M. E., & Benson, H. (1989). The efficacy of the relaxation response in preparing for cardiac surgery. *Behavioral Medicine, 15*(3), 111–17.

Lipton, L., & Wellman, B., with Humbard, C. (2003). *Mentoring matters: A practical guide to learning-focused relationships* (2nd ed.). Sherman, CT: MiraVia.

Lortie, D. C. (1977). *Schoolteacher: A sociological study.* Chicago: University of Chicago Press.

Markland, D., & Hardy, L. (1993). Anxiety, relaxation and anaesthesia for day-case surgery. *British Journal of Clinical Psychology, 32,* 493–504.

Marshall, J. D., Smagorinsky, P., & Smith, M. W. (1995). *The language of interpretation: Patterns of discourse in discussions of literature.* Urbana, IL: National Council of Teachers of English.

McCann, T. M. (2001). What makes novice teachers cry and what can we do to help? *California English, 6*(4), 24–27.

McCann, T. M., & Johannessen, L. R. (2004). Why do new teachers cry? *The Clearing House, 77*(4), 138–45.

McCann, T. M., Johannessen, L. R., & Ricca, P. B. (2004, Spring). Why do teachers leave, and what can we do to keep them? *HOT TOPICS, 40*. Illinois Association for Supervision and Curriculum Development. Retrieved January 28, 2005, from www.illinoisascd.com/hot topics.html.

McCann, T. M., Johannessen, L. R., & Ricca, B. P. (in press). Supporting and keeping new teachers. *Educational Leadership.*

Merrow, J. (1999, October 6). The teacher shortage: Wrong diagnosis, phony cures. *Education Week*, 38, 64.

National Commission on Teaching and America's Future. (2003). *No dream denied: A pledge to America's children.* Washington, DC: Author.

National Council of Teachers of English and International Reading Association. (1996). *Standards for the English language arts.* Urbana, IL, and Newark, DE: Authors.

Nystrand, M., with Gamoran, A., Kachur, R., & Prendergast, C. (1997). *Opening dialogue: Understanding the dynamics of language and learning in the English classroom.* New York: Teachers College Press.

O'Neill, T., with Novak, W. (1987). *Man of the House: The life and political memoirs of Speaker Tip O'Neill.* New York: Random House.

Perez, K., Swain, C., & Hartsough, C. S. (1997). Teacher mentoring and teacher retention. *Journal of Teacher Education, 43*(3), 200–204.

Popham, W. J. (2003). *Test better, teach better: The instructional role of assessment.* Alexandria, VA: Association for Supervision and Curriculum Development.

Rominger, L. M., Packard, S., & Elkin, N. (2001). *Your first year as a high school teacher: Making the transition from a total novice to a successful professional.* Roseville, CA: Prima.

Rumelhart, D. E. (1980). Schemata: The building blocks of cognition. In R. J. Spiro, B. C. Bruce, & W. F. Brewer (Eds.), *Theoretical issues in reading and comprehension: Perspectives from cognitive psychology, linguistics, artificial intelligence, and education.* Hillsdale, NJ: Erlbaum.

Rutherford, W. L., & Hall, G. E. (1990). *Concerns of teachers: Revisiting the original theory after twenty years.* Paper presented at the annual meeting of the American Educational Research Association, Boston.

Scholes, R. (1998). *The rise and fall of English: Reconstructing English as a discipline*. New Haven: Yale University Press.

Smagorinsky, P. (2002). *Teaching English through principled practice*. Upper Saddle River, NJ: Merrill Prentice Hall.

Smagorinsky, P. (2004). *Virtual library of conceptual units*. Retrieved March 18, 2005, from http://www.coe.uga.edu/~smago/VirtualLibrary.

Smagorinsky, P., & Whiting, M. E. (1995). *How English teachers get taught: Methods of teaching the methods class*. Urbana, IL: National Council of Teachers of English.

Small, R. C., Jr., & Strzepek, J. E. (1988). *A casebook for English teachers: Dilemmas and decisions*. Belmont, CA: Wadsworth.

Snyder, T. D., & Hoffman, C. H. (2003). *Digest of education statistics 2002*. Washington, DC: Office of Educational Research and Improvement, National Center for Education Statistics, U.S. Department of Education. (NCES 2003-060)

Stanford, G. (Ed.). (1979). *How to handle the paper load*. Urbana, IL: National Council of Teachers of English.

Stuart, J. (1970). *The thread that runs so true*. New York: Scribner.

Texas State Board of Education. (1998). *Texas State Board for Educator Certification Panel on Novice Teacher Induction Support System: Final report*. Austin: Author.

Veenman, S. (1984). Perceived problems of beginning teachers. *Review of Educational Research, 54*(2), 143–78.

Villani, S. (2002). *Mentoring programs for new teachers: Models of induction and support*. Thousand Oaks, CA: Corwin Press.

Vonnegut, K. (1965). *God bless you, Mr. Rosewater: Or, pearls before swine*. New York: Dell.

Wagner, B. J., & Larson, M. (1995). *Situations: A casebook of virtual realities for the English teacher*. Portsmouth, NH: Boynton/Cook.

Wayne, A. J. (2000). Teacher supply and demand: Surprises from primary research. *Education Policy Analysis Archives, 8*(47).

Whitener, S. D., Gruber, K. J., Lynch, H., Tingos, K., Perona, M., & Fondelier, S. (1997). *Characteristics of stayers, movers, and leavers: Results from the teacher followup survey, 1994–95*. Washington, DC: Office of Educational Research and Improvement, Center for Education Statistics, U.S. Department of Education.

Whyte, W. F. (1948). *Human relations in the restaurant industry.* New York: McGraw-Hill.

Wiggins, G., & McTighe, J. (1998). *Understanding by design.* Alexandria, VA: Association for Supervision and Curriculum Development.

Wong, H. K., & Wong, R. T. (1999). *The first days of school: How to be an effective teacher* (2nd ed.). Mountain View, CA: Harry K. Wong Publications.

Yancey, K. B. (Ed.). (1992). *Portfolios in the writing classroom: An introduction.* Urbana, IL: National Council of Teachers of English.

INDEX

Administrative relationships, 4,
23, 29–31, 77, 83–84,
116–17, 144–46, 161. *See
also* Evaluation of
teachers
experienced teacher's
perspective, 88, 91–92
proactive help in crises, 125–26
Advice
for administration, 77, 83–84,
120–27 (*See also* Administrative relationships)
for new teachers, 82–83 (*See
also* Novice teachers)
for teacher training programs,
78, 127–30 (*See also*
Teacher training
programs)
Attitudes, survey of, 44–47
Attrition, 1–7
fiscal cost of, 4
impact of shortages, 2–3
Autonomy issues, 16, 19, 45, 46,
50, 136, 153–55
experienced teacher's
perspective, 88

Casebooks, 128, 129–30
Case studies, 13
critical times, 64–65, 75–76,
193–94
gender issues, 25–27
novice teacher concerns, 24–31
one-year follow-up, 78–80

physical/personal charac-
teristics of teachers, 25–27
race considerations, 28–31
responses to school opening,
63–64
returning after winter break,
68–69
teachers and teaching
contexts, 61–63
for teacher training, 111
Classroom management, 4, 6,
17, 18, 21–22, 30, 49, 76
activities, 45, 51, 75
decision making, 4
experienced teacher's
perspective, 87, 88
orderly discussions, 75
Cluster analysis, 52, 54n. 2
demographics and, 52
experienced teachers, 53
novice teachers, 53
Collaboration, 69–70, 77
Colleague relationships, 17, 18,
45, 46, 73–74, 84, 107–9,
123–24, 142–44
support staff, 143–44
talking to peers, 115–16, 123–
24
Conceptual memos, 9, 15, 60
Confidence, 19, 81
in addressing colleagues, 107–9
preservice versus practicing, 45
Contract issues, 106–7
Control issues, 16, 19, 153–55.
See also Autonomy issues

Coping strategies, 31–33
Critical times, 13, 48, 64–65,
    75–76, 193–94
Curriculum, 16, 19, 70, 133,
    148–51
  experienced teacher's
    perspective, 93–94
  guides, 150
  underlying principles, 104
Cycle of school year, 147, 193–94
  critical times, 64–65, 75–76
  responses to school opening,
    63–64, 193
  returning after winter break,
    68–69

Darling-Hammond, L., 3, 55
Department chairs, 71, 84
Diederich, Paul, 151
District policies, 5

English teacher, path to
    becoming, 118
Enriched students, 80
Erickson, F., 9
ESL training, 70, 77
Evaluation of teachers, 16, 19,
    30, 66–67, 71, 109–10.
    See also Administrative
    relationships
  experienced teacher's
    perspective, 88, 92, 109–
    10
  observation, 125
  professional conversations,
    125
  professional development versus
    punishment, 124–25
Expectations versus experience,
    21, 44, 45, 158
Experienced teachers, 86–97
  classroom management, 87, 88
  cluster analysis, 53
  curriculum ideas of, 93–94
  grading of students, 88–89
  options of, 102
  physical/personal
    characteristics of teachers,
    88, 95–97
  responses to difficult
    scenarios, 98–117
  responses to evaluation, 88,
    92, 109–10
  response to workload, 88–89
  student relationships, 87, 88
  trends among, 15
  using theory, 101–2
Extracurricular activities, 75, 76

Factor analysis, 45, 47, 54n. 1
Fatigue factor, 47–50, 65–68, 121,
    161. *See also* Workload
First-year teachers. *See* Novice
    teachers
Fringe benefits, 5
Fuller, F. F., 6

Gender issues, 9, 25–27, 66
God Bless You, Mr. Rosewater
    (Vonnegut), 137
Grading of students, 16, 18, 45,
    46, 51–52, 52, 67–68, 69,
    151–53
  commentary, 152
  doubts about, 50
  experienced teacher's
    perspective, 88–89
  grading essays, 35–36, 74, 152
  summary grades, 49
  tests, 152
Grossman, P., 5

Hall, G. E., 6
Hartsough, C. S., 3
Harvard Business School, 111
Hillocks, G., Jr., 154
Hussar, W. J., 3, 4

Induction into teaching, 119, 121, 122–23, 164
Information overload, 77
Ingersoll, R. M., 3, 4, 120
Inquiry frame, 112
Inservice training, 122–23
International Reading Association, 154
Interview protocol, 112
Interviews. *See also* Research questions and methods; Surveys
conceptual memos, 9, 15, 60
of experienced teachers, 111–13, 195–97
first-year teachers, 56–60
follow-up, 11–13, 34, 60, 78–80, 178–79
gender of participants, 9
generalization about beginning teachers, 1–2
initial interviews, 8–10
novice teacher questions, 167
questions, 9
readers, 9–10
research questions and methods, 6–7, 8–10, 11–13
as therapeutic, 73, 124
Isolation, 23–24, 43

Job dissatisfaction, 4, 37
Job security, 37
Johnson, S. M., 31

Literature selections, 51. *See also* Subject knowledge
Lortie, D. C., 43

McTighe, J., 149
Media images of teaching, 47
Mentoring
designing program, 122
dysfunctional, 114

mentor training, 122
novice teachers, 37, 40, 43, 48, 69, 72, 83, 113–15, 119, 121–22, 161
student teachers, 131–32
Mission, 39

National Council of Teachers of English (NCTE), 117, 126, 154
National Council of Teachers of English (NCTE) Annual Convention, 79
NCTE Leadership Development Award, 79
No Child Left Behind, 153
Novice teachers. *See also specific topics*
balancing personal life and job demands, 36–37
cluster analysis, 53
concerns of, 6, 16–33
definition of, 8
doubts, 50
frustrations of, 6
imitating experienced teacher practices, 161–62 (*See also* Experienced teachers)
pattern of experience, 55–85
resources available to, 7
responses to difficult scenarios, 98–117
self-definition issues, 6, 19 (*See also* Teacher persona)
self-help, 119, 136–57
surveys, 10–11
those likely to continue teaching, 35, 38–41
those unlikely to continue teaching, 34–38

O'Neill, Thomas "Tip," 1
Orientation, 122–23. *See also* Induction into teaching

Paper grading, 35–36, 74, 152.
    See also Workload
Paper load, 58, 67–68
Parent relationships, 17, 18, 27,
    28–29, 45, 46, 80, 102–3,
    140–42
Partnerships. *See* University
    partnership with high
    schools
Patterns of change, 86–87
Patterns of experience, 13
Peer mediation, 106
Perez, K., 3
Physical demands of teaching,
    76. *See also* Fatigue factor
Physical/personal characteristics
    of teachers, 16, 19, 45,
    46, 50, 156–57
    case study, 25–27
    experienced teacher's
        perspective, 88, 95–97
Popham, W. J., 152
Popularity, 76
Preservice teachers. *See also*
    Novice teachers
    conversations with
        experienced teachers,
        111–13, 129
    freedom concerns, 6
    surveys, 10–11
    workload ideas, 45
Problem-based scenarios, 98–
    117, 164, 198
    experienced teachers, 185–92
    novice teachers, 180–84
Problem situations, 15
Professional community, 117,
    126–27

Race considerations, 28–31
Recruitment, 3
Relationships, 16. *See also*
    Administrative
    relationships; Colleague
    relationships; Parent
    relationships; Student
    relationships
Research questions and methods,
    6–7. *See also* Interviews;
    Surveys
    directions for future research,
        163–65
    follow-up interviews, 11–13
    high school settings, 9–10
    initial interviews, 8–10
    procedures, 8
    schedule of visits for first-year
        teachers, 14
Retention, 164–65
    support for, 118–20
    versus recruitment, 3, 55
Rutherford, W. L., 6

Salaries, 5, 49, 119
Scholes, R., 104
School culture, 24, 26–27, 131–
    32
Self-definition issues, 6
Smagorinsky, P., 154
Smith, T. M., 3, 4
Special ed students, 80
Special ed training, 70, 77
Staff development, 122–23
State learning standards for
    English language arts, 154
Stress and stress management,
    10, 31–33. *See also*
    Workload
Student-centered instruction, 76
    negotiation, 139
    rapport, 139
Student relationships, 16, 18,
    45, 137–40, 160–61
    apathy, 36
    discipline, 4, 51, 69 (*See also*
        Classroom management)
    experienced teacher's
        perspective, 87, 88
    student-centered activities, 76
    student motivation, 4

talking down to students, 76
unresponsive classes, 20–21
Student teaching, 40, 48, 55
placements, 131–32
Subject knowledge, 16, 19, 45, 46,
51, 104–5, 136, 148–51
"big ideas," 149
construction of meaning, 150
"pathfinder" metaphor, 105
transmission model of
instruction, 149
Supervisors. *See* Administrative
relationships
Support systems, 4, 26–27, 73–
74, 123–24. *See also*
Administrative
relationships; Colleague
relationships
collegial contacts, 123–24
external resource person, 123–
24
Surveys. *See also* Research
questions and methods
attitude, 44–47
formation of, 10–11
practicing teacher, 10–11
preservice, 10–11
reliability of, 11
teacher expectation survey,
10–11, 44, 168–72
teacher experience surveys, 10,
11, 44, 173–77
validity of, 11
variance in, 45
Swain, C., 3

Teacher Expectation Survey, 10–
11, 44, 168–72
Teacher Experience Survey, 10–
11, 44, 173–77
Teacher motivations, 38–39
Teacher persona, 17, 27, 130–
31, 158, 159–60
Teachers. *See* Experienced
teachers; Novice teachers

Teacher shortages, 2–3
demographics, 2
Teacher training programs, 48,
70, 78, 84, 127–30. *See
also* Theory versus
practice; University
partnership with high
schools
conversations with
experienced teachers,
111–13, 129
"fast track" system, 55
helping student develop
persona, 159–60
immersion, 110–11, 130–31
maintaining contact after
graduation, 128–29, 134–
35
medical analogy, 55–56
teaching problem-solving
skills, 127–28, 133
Teacher turnover, 4, 5
Teaching assignments, 5, 120–21
minimal classroom changes for
new teachers, 120–21
minimal preparation for new
teachers, 120–21
survival-of-the-fittest
rationale, 121
Teaching skills, 39
Teenagers, 76
Tests, 152
Texas Teacher Certification
Board, 4
Theory versus practice, 40, 101–
2, 129–30, 133–34
Thompson, C., 5
Time management, 16, 40. *See
also* Workload
Transmission model of
instruction, 149

University partnership with high
schools, 119, 130–35,
158–59

Valencia, S., 5
Vonnegut, Kurt, 137
Vulnerable times. *See* Critical
    times

Whitener, S. D., 4
Whyte, W. F., 1–2
Wiggins, G., 149
Wong, H. K., 136
Wong, R. T., 136
Workload, 16, 18, 31–32, 40, 43,
    45, 46, 47, 136, 146–48

experienced teacher's
    perspective, 88–89
grading essays, 35–36, 74, 152
perceived as unreasonable, 34–
    36
preservice teachers
    expectations of, 45 (*See
    also* Expectations versus
    experience)

Youngs, P., 55

AUTHORS

Thomas M. McCann has taught English in a variety of school settings, including eight years in an alternative school. He holds a BA degree from Northern Illinois University, an MA from Southern Illinois University, an MA from Saint Xavier University, and a PhD from the University of Chicago. He has published articles in *Research in the Teaching of English*, *English Journal*, *Illinois English Bulletin*, and *California English*. With Peter Smagorinsky and Stephen Kern, he is the coauthor of *Explorations: Introductory Activities for Literature and Composition, 7–12* (1987). With Larry R. Johannessen, he is the coauthor of *In Case You Teach English: An Interactive Casebook for Prospective and Practicing Teachers* (2002). He has taught in four high schools, two colleges, and three universities, where he worked with preservice and practicing teachers in graduate education programs. McCann has supervised teachers in high school for twenty years. He served for fourteen years as English department chair at Community High School in West Chicago, Illinois, where he taught English and supervised other English teachers. He is now assistant superintendent for curriculum and instruction at Elmhurst Public Schools. He also serves as adjunct professor of English at Elmhurst College. He lives in Elmhurst, Illinois, with his wife Pamela and daughter Katie.

Larry R. Johannessen is associate professor in the Department of English at Northern Illinois University, where he teaches in the English education program as well as literature courses primarily dealing with the Vietnam War. He holds a BA from California State University, Hayward, and an MAT and a PhD from the University of Chicago. He taught high school English and history for ten years. In addition to chapters in books, he has contributed over sixty articles to scholarly journals. He is author of *Illumination Rounds: Teaching the Literature of the Vietnam War* (1992) and coauthor of two popular NCTE publications: *Writing about Literature* (1984) and *Designing and Sequencing Prewriting Activities* (1982). Johannessen is listed in *Who's Who Among America's Teachers* and *Who's Who in American Education*. His current research is in the areas of teacher knowledge and thinking, particularly for preservice and novice teachers; secondary school English curriculum and instruction; literacy learning; and the literature and film of the Vietnam War. He lives in Wheaton, Illinois, with his wife, Elizabeth Kahn.

Bernard P. Ricca is assistant professor in the School of Education at Dominican University. He holds a BA from the University of Dallas, an MA from the University of Chicago, and a PhD from the University of Michigan. He has taught high school in Texas and Illinois, and is a frequent inservice presenter, particularly on integrating technology into the classroom. In addition to book chapters and journal articles, he is the author of *Teaching about the Physics of Sports* (2001). His research interests include student conceptual change and teacher preparation and support. He lives in Franklin Park, Illinois, with his wife, Stephanie Townsend.

This book was typeset in Sabon by Electronic Imaging.
Typefaces used on the cover were Handel Gothic and Frutiger.
The book was printed on 60-lb. Accent Opaque paper by Versa Press, Inc.